The A–Z Guide to Working in Further Education

Jonathan Gravells
Susan Wallace

A-Z
GUIDES

You might also like the following books in our *Further Education* series

A Complete Guide to the Level 4 Certificate in Education and Training
By Lynn Machin, Duncan Hindmarch, Sandra Murray and Tina Richardson
978-1-909330-89-4
September 2013

Understanding the Further Education Sector: A critical guide to policies and practices
By Susan Wallace
978-1-909330-21-4
September 2013

Dial M for Mentor: Critical reflections on mentoring for coaches, educators and trainers
By Jonathan Gravells and Susan Wallace
978-1-909330-00-9
In print

Most of our titles are also available in a range of electronic formats. To order please go to our website www.criticalpublishing.com or contact our distributor, NBN International, 10 Thornbury Road, Plymouth PL6 7PP, telephone 01752 202301 or email orders@nbninternational.com.

The A–Z Guide to Working in Further Education

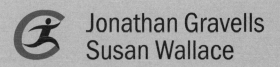

Jonathan Gravells
Susan Wallace

A-Z
GUIDES

First published in 2013 by Critical Publishing Ltd

British Library Cataloguing in Publication Data
A CIP record for this book is available from the British Library

ISBN: 978-1-909330-85-6

This book is also available in the following e-book formats:
Kindle ISBN: 978-1-909330-86-3
EPUB ISBN: 978-1-909330-87-0
Adobe e-book ISBN: 978-1-909330-88-7

Cover design by Greensplash Limited
Project Management by Out of House Publishing
Printed and bound in Great Britain by T J International

Critical Publishing
152 Chester Road
Northwich
CW8 4AL
www.criticalpublishing.com

MIX
Paper from responsible sources
FSC   FSC® C018575
www.fsc.org

Contents

	List of themes	*viii*
	Organisational chart of Bogginbrook College	*xiii*
	Meet the authors	*xv*
	Introduction	1
A is for:	Adult Learners	2
	Annual Review/Appraisal	5
	APL/APEL	9
	Assessment	10
	Authenticity	12
B is for:	Behaviour Management	14
	Benchmarking	16
	Bullying	17
C is for:	Challenging	20
	Change	22
	The Cinderella Sector	26
	Coaching	27
	Conflict	32
	Consult or Control	35
	Critical Thinking	37
	Curriculum	39
D is for:	Delegation	40
	Disciplinary	43
	Diversity	45
E is for:	Emotional Intelligence	46
	Employability Skills	48
	Engagement 1	50
	Engagement 2	51
	ETF	55
F is for:	Feedback	56
	Foster Report	58

G is for:	Grading	59
H is for:	HE in FE	60
	Human Resources	62
I is for:	Inclusion	64
	Influencing	66
	Inspection	70
	Interviews	72
J is for:	JFDI	77
K is for:	Kinaesthetic Learners	79
L is for:	Leadership	80
	Learning Outcomes	83
	Lesson Planning	85
	Listening	87
M is for:	Managing Upwards	90
	Market	93
	Meetings	95
	Mentoring	98
	Mission Statement	106
	Motivation	107
N is for:	Negotiation	109
O is for:	Objectives	113
	Observations	115
P is for:	Paperwork	117
	Performance Management	118
	Politics	121
	Professionalism	124
Q is for:	Quality	125
R is for:	Recruitment	126
	Reflective Practice	128
	Resilience	130
	Respect	133
S is for:	Seating	135
	Selection	137

	Silver Book	142
	Stress	143
	Styles of Learning	147
T is for:	Taking Responsibility	148
	Teamwork	151
	Time Management	155
	Trust	159
U is for:	Updating	162
V is for:	Vice Principal	164
	VLEs and Other Learning Technologies	165
W is for:	Walking Around	167
	White Papers and Other Milestones	169
X is for:	X-Men	171
Y is for:	You	172
Z is for:	Zero-Tolerance	173
And Finally	P is for Postscript	174
	Useful references	*175*
	Useful websites	*178*
	Useful sources for updating	*179*

List of themes

Being an excellent teacher

A is for Assessment

B is for Behaviour Management

C is for Critical Thinking

C is for Curriculum

E is for Employability Skills

I is for Inclusion

L is for Learning Outcomes

L is for Lesson Planning

O is for Observations

P is for Professionalism

R is for Reflective Practice

S is for Seating

Supporting learners and their learning

A is for Adult Learners

A is for APL/APEL

D is for Diversity

E is for Emotional Intelligence

E is for Engagement

F is for Feedback

G is for Grading

H is for HE in FE

I is for Inclusion

K is for Kinaesthetic Learners

L is for Listening

M is for Motivation

R is for Respect

S is for Styles of Learning

V is for VLEs and Other Learning Technologies

College matters

A is for Annual Review/Appraisal

B is for Benchmarking

B is for Bullying

D is for Disciplinary

D is for Diversity

G is for Grading

M is for Market

M is for Mission Statement

R is for Recruitment

S is for Selection

T is for Taking Responsibility

The FE and training context

C is for the Cinderella Sector

E is for ETF

F is for the Foster Report

I is for Inspection

M is for Market

V is for Vice Principal

W is for White Papers and Other Milestones

Personal effectiveness

D is for Delegation

J is for JFDI

M is for Managing Upwards

M is for Meetings

O is for Objectives

P is for Paperwork

R is for Resilience

S is for Stress

T is for Taking Responsibility

T is for Time Management

T is for Trust

Making the most of change

C is for Change

J is for JFDI

R is for Resilience

S is for Stress

T is for Taking Responsibility

U is for Updating

Taking the lead

A is for Authenticity

B is for Bullying

C is for Consult or Control

E is for Emotional Intelligence

L is for Leadership

O is for Objectives

R is for Respect

T is for Taking Responsibility

W is for Walking Around

X is for X-Men

Z is for Zero-Tolerance

Developing your communication skills

A is for Annual Review/Appraisal

A is for Authenticity

C is for Challenging

C is for Coaching

E is for Emotional Intelligence

I is for Interviews

L is for Listening

M is for Mentoring

N is for Negotiation

P is for Politics

CPD: improving performance

A is for Annual Review/Appraisal

C is for Coaching

F is for Feedback

I is for Interviews

M is for Mentoring

P is for Performance Management

U is for Updating

Developing resilience, reducing stress

B is for Bullying

M is for Managing Upwards

M is for Mentoring

P is for Paperwork

P is for Politics

R is for Resilience

S is for Stress

T is for Time Management

Y is for You

Z is for Zero-Tolerance

Organisational Chart of Bogginbrook College
(showing in BOLD the managers who play a role in the A–Z)

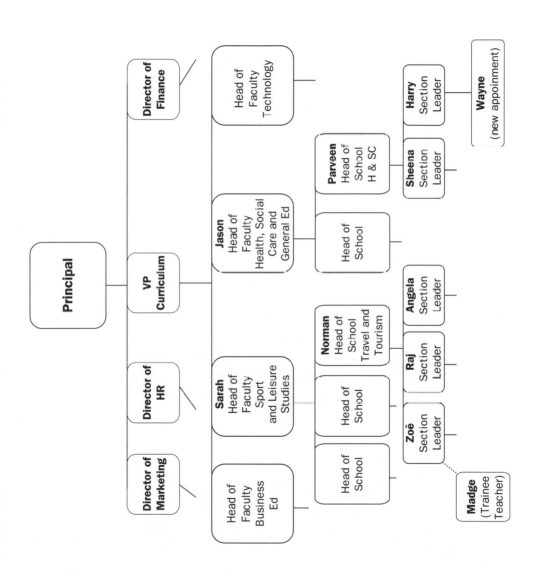

Meet the authors

Jonathan Gravells

I am a management consultant who advises organisations on mentoring and coaching, providing corporate training in the UK and around the world. I have published widely on mentoring, leadership and personal change. I am a Fellow of the Chartered Institute of Personnel and Development, a member of the European Mentoring and Coaching Council, and on the NHS register of approved executive coaches.

Susan Wallace

I am the Professor of Continuing Education at Nottingham Trent University, and part of my role is to support learning on the initial training courses for teachers in the further education sector. I taught in the sector myself for ten years, including on BTEC programmes and Basic Skills provision. My particular interest is in the motivation and behaviour of students in further education, and in mentoring and the ways in which a successful mentoring relationship can support personal and professional development. I have also written a number of popular books for teachers and student teachers in the sector. One aspect of this that I particularly enjoy is that it gives me opportunities to get to know lots of people, either from e-mails or in the colleges that I visit, whom I wouldn't otherwise meet.

Introduction

Welcome to this A–Z!

Whether you've just been appointed to your first job in further education (FE), or you're a trainee teacher starting out on your career, or you've been promoted to a leadership or management role and are wanting a quick update, this book is for you. You'll find that you can use it in a number of ways. You may like simply to dip into it to discover a definition, or to mug up on a particular topic prior to a meeting. Or you may like to do some more concentrated reading with a specific focus by following linked entries to explore one of the themes, such as *Improving Performance* or *Making the Most of Change*, which we've mapped out for you on the previous pages. Perhaps you'll use it to refresh your memory about lesson planning, or management theory, or even to remind yourself about the funny side of working in FE.

In your reading of this A–Z you'll encounter certain characters who appear and reappear in the various examples and scenarios. As FE trainees and professionals they all have their strengths and foibles, and we hope that the process of spotting these will add to your enjoyment of the book. They are there to instruct (by good example or otherwise), but also to entertain. Their triumphs, quandaries and disasters all take place at Bogginbrook College – an entirely fictional institution. We provide an organisational chart at the beginning of this book so that you can see at a glance how these characters relate to one another in their management roles.

For whatever purpose you use this A–Z – and we hope you find it helpful in all the ways we've mentioned – do bear in mind that it's intended primarily as a toolkit for busy teachers, trainee teachers, leaders and managers. It makes no claim to be an in-depth textbook. The individual entries are designed to provide rule-of-thumb advice on practical matters, or working summaries of relevant theory. The list of themes allows you to take your exploration one step further; as do the cross-references, indicated in bold. But if you'd like to pursue any of these topics or ideas in more depth, you'll find suggestions for further reading incorporated in the text, as well as summarised in the Useful References section at the end of the book.

A is for Adult Learners

Madge is a trainee FE teacher based at Bogginbrook College. The content of the training sessions she has attended so far has been heavily focused on supporting the learning of 16–19-year-olds, so she is rather alarmed to discover that one group of learners she'll be working with as part of her practical teaching experience is *entirely composed* of adult learners, all aged over 25. She rushes off to find her mentor, Zoe, to ask for help.

MADGE: *Help!*

ZOE: *Come on, Madge, it's absolutely nothing to worry about. Teaching adults is really enjoyable. And they're a lovely group. I thought you'd like to broaden your experience a bit.*

MADGE: *But some of them will be older than me! They won't want to listen to me! They'll know more than me!*

ZOE: *Just stop panicking and take a deep breath. I'll tell you a bit about adult learners, OK? And then you can tell me whether you still feel the same. First of all, they're often not as confident as they appear. Returning to education or training after a long time outside it can feel quite daunting. Some haven't sat in front of a teacher since they were at school. And if their experience of school was about feeling a failure, you can imagine how nervous they might be when they come to college. So part of your job is to reassure them and put them at ease. Some of them will be much more nervous of you than you are of them. The second thing to remember is that, as adults, they'll have responsibilities and commitments outside college – much more so than younger students; and sometimes those things will take priority. So you have to be prepared to be flexible. And thirdly, those other commitments mean that they'll expect good value for the time commitment they're making in coming to college. That is, they tend to be more goal-oriented than younger learners. They need you to provide a clear structure and learning experiences that keep them on their toes. If you remember those three things, you'll find teaching adults a real pleasure.*

MADGE: *So they'll be more nervous of me than I will of them?*

ZOE: *Some of them, yes, at first. But you'll need to put them at ease, otherwise they'll not be able to learn effectively. Remember your Maslow?*

Here are some other pointers that Zoe will probably give Madge when the time is right.

> » Be sure to provide your adult learners with a clear programme or schedule of sessions, and then stick to it. Adults have busy lives and multiple responsibilities, and need to know about key dates and deadlines well ahead of time.

» Always start on time and never finish early. Adult learners will have invested precious time and money, and may have made complicated arrangements in order to be able to attend. They won't appreciate late starts or truncated sessions.

» Choose your methods carefully. Adult learners may be keener to get down to business than their younger counterparts, and will therefore appreciate time-effective methods and plenty of teacher input. They need to leave your lesson feeling that every minute of their precious time has been spent usefully.

» Always communicate with them adult to adult. For example, avoid giving praise in a way that sounds patronising. *Good. Yes. Thank you* is clearly much preferable to *Well done! Clever girl!*

» Think carefully about rules for behaviour. For example, demanding that adults raise their hand to answer a question could be seen as inappropriate; whereas requiring a certain level of respect in classroom interactions is entirely reasonable.

» Madge's biggest nightmare seems to be that some of the learners will be older than she is. But this can be used to real advantage. A group of adult learners provides a vast range of work and life experience on which a teacher can draw. So always remember that adult learners can in themselves be a valuable *learning* resource.

» If you do find that you are youngest in the room, it's fine to acknowledge that you're aware of that. You can introduce topics with phrases such as, *Here's something some of you will already be aware of.* Or, *As some of you will know better than I do ...* In this way you avoid presenting yourself as the only source of expertise, and show that you are prepared to defer to another's detailed knowledge or experience. This is part of building a mutually respectful working relationship.

» Don't demand that your adult learners jump through unnecessary hoops. This will only alienate them. For example, insisting that a mother of six learns to bath a baby by watching you wash a plastic doll is not going to convince her she's making good use of her time. So get her to the front and let her do the demonstration instead of you.

Zoe makes reference to Abraham Maslow (1908–70), an American psychologist whose theory of a *hierarchy of needs* is often used to explain issues around people's motivation to learn. According to Maslow, our basic needs for safety and a sense of security must be met before we can aspire to fulfil our higher needs such as learning and achieving our full potential as a human being (which Maslow calls *self-actualisation*).

Further reading

To find out more about teaching adults you could read:

Rogers, A. and Horrocks, N. (2010) *Teaching Adults* (4th Edition). Maidenhead: Open University Press.

To find out more about Maslow's *hierarchy of needs* you could read:

Maslow, A. (1987) *Motivation and Personality*. London: Harper & Row.

A is for Annual Review/Appraisal

What thoughts go through your mind when you see the title of this section? Excitement? Eager anticipation? Unbridled joy? Possibly not. Research tells us that many managers find this annual task about as appealing as unblocking a drain. So it is probably safe to assume that their staff may not all look forward to the occasion with relish either. Yet it is still likely these days in FE that you will be called upon to participate in formal annual reviews or appraisals, both as an appraiser and as an appraisee. So, whatever your role, how can you make this a meaningful and productive conversation?

First let us consider why an appraisal produces this sinking feeling in the first place. A number of explanations spring to mind.

> » Many of us have suffered at the hands of line managers or team leaders who do this badly.

> » We are all a little frightened about giving (and receiving) feedback.

> » For some, this is the only time that performance is discussed, and it therefore becomes a huge and daunting task.

> » We worry about our ability to control the conversation and the emotions it may release, particularly if we've been hearing rumours about performance-related pay.

> » It can feel like a confrontation and these are always easier to avoid than to face up to.

Understandable though these feelings are, all of us like to know how we are getting on, what the organisation and/or our own manager expects of us, and how we are going to learn and develop in our chosen career path. So, if you are a manager, you may find yourself laying claim to all sorts of alternative strategies:

> » *I speak to my staff every day, on an informal basis* (translation: *I'm frightened of doing appraisals*);

> » *I review targets on a regular basis at team meetings* (translation: *I'm frightened of doing appraisals, but I like to crack the whip*);

> » *my team are all experienced professionals. They know what they need to do* (translation: *I won't take responsibility for being in charge, and I can't be bothered to agree objectives ... Oh, and I'm frightened of doing appraisals*).

Feeling more comfortable with the formal appraisal process requires three things:

1.   a clear understanding of why it's important;
2.   the skills to handle the process competently and confidently;
3.   an integrated approach to performance management, which sets the appraisal 'event' in a wider framework of management activity (see **P is for Performance Management**).

Since the appraisal should be a two-way process, we can look at why it's important from two points of view:

The APPRAISER wants:

» to reinforce good performance and positive behaviour on the part of the appraisee;

» to jointly identify and resolve any problems in the appraisee's performance;

» to agree objectives which

– enable the appraisee to contribute fully to the future objectives of the college and the team;

– enable the appraisee to develop and grow appropriately in their role;

» to leave the appraisee feeling motivated;

» to improve or consolidate their relationship with the appraisee;

» to get feedback on their own behaviour and performance.

The APPRAISEE wants:

» to know where he/she stands, how they are doing;

» to know how their contribution is valued;

» to be congratulated where they have done well;

» to find out what's coming up and what is expected of them;

» to resolve any lingering frustrations in doing their job;

» to agree how they can learn and develop.

It's true that most of these outcomes can also be achieved through more frequent coaching sessions, provided these are regular and properly structured (see **C is for Coaching**). In this case, the appraisal can become more of an opportunity to take stock of the year, formally recognise achievements, and agree long-term objectives and personal development plans. When performance is continuously monitored and discussed in this way, it immediately removes one of our earlier barriers to appraisal. It's no longer such a huge and daunting task for either party. The formal appraisal conversation is unlikely to hold any surprises, as instances of good or unsatisfactory performance will have been discussed nearer the time they occurred. You may not be in a position to decide when and how formal appraisals are carried out, but you can choose to make these just one part of a staff development approach that also incorporates more frequent, coaching conversations.

So what skills do we need? In essence, they are the skills of any interview (see **I is for Interviews**), including rapport-building, listening, questioning, summarising, etc. As with any interview PREPARATION by both parties is important.

As APPRAISER:

» think about what the appraisee has done well/struggled with. Have examples ready;

» gather any necessary documentation (forms, booklets, guidance notes, last year's documents, evidence to support performance assessment);

» ensure you are familiar with any key standards (such as national standards for teaching in the Lifelong Learning sector), the appraisal scheme of the college if there is one;

» consider the training and development needs of the appraisee;

» look at your objectives for the coming year and think about what the appraisee could do;

» seek views on the appraisee from colleagues and other appropriate people;

» agree a suitable time, date and venue. (Make adequate space. This is not a half-hour job and the meeting should not be interrupted.);

» think what might be on the the appraisee's agenda. Why not ask them?;

» discuss all this with *your* manager;

» make sure the appraisee understands the review or appraisal process fully and check that they, too, have prepared.

As APPRAISEE:

» look at what you have achieved in the past year. Relate it to your objectives and to those of the team and college as a whole;

» what aspects of your job are you best at?;

» consider what changes might help you do a better job (your skills/know-ledge, your relationships, resources, responsibilities, etc. These will also include your CPD needs);

» are there any aspects of your role on which you need further clarification?;

» are there other ways in which you could contribute to the team/college, and what support would you need to do this?;

» do you have longer-term career plans? If so, what are they and how will you achieve them?

The approach to the actual appraisal discussion should be one of joint problem-solving and planning (*What can we do to help you develop and perform even better?*). The appraisee should do 70 per cent of the talking. In this respect it is very much a coaching dialogue (see **C is for Coaching**).

Other key skills needed for an effective appraisal discussion are giving and receiving feedback and jointly devising SMART objectives. You can read more about this in our sections, **F is for Feedback** and **O is for Objectives**.

As for linking appraisal outcomes directly to pay, opinion in FE remains divided between those who see it as destructive, inhibiting open discussion and buy-in to self-development, and those who believe the financial incentive is vital to an integrated performance management approach. It's interesting to reflect, however, that at an organisational level the college itself is funded largely according to performance.

A is for APL/APEL

Accreditation of Prior Learning (APL) and Accreditation of Prior Experience and Learning (APEL) are terms used to describe the process of awarding credits which can be counted towards a qualification, based on the learner's previous qualifications, learning or experience. This method of accreditation was made possible by the competence-based structure of National Vocational Qualifications (NVQs), which allows for assessment to be based on the learner's current competence independently of whether they have completed a specific course or examination. Learners applying for accreditation are usually required to present a portfolio of evidence which will contain things such as previously gained certificates, observer reports, witness statements, and photographs or examples of their work. The portfolio is then evaluated by a qualified assessor and a decision made as to the extent of the credit to be awarded. It is technically possible to achieve an entire qualification in this way; but it is more usual for APL/APEL candidates to be accredited upfront with one or more units of the qualification for which they are enrolling, so that they only have to be assessed on those remaining. Sometimes, however, the fee for taking the APL/APEL route makes it more expensive for the learner than simply enrolling for the whole qualification.

A is for Assessment

Wayne is a newly qualified teacher and is about to take in his first batch of level 2 assignments. He's feeling a bit nervous about this because it's the first time he'll be responsible for assessing learners' written work. So he goes to have a word with Harry, his section leader.

HARRY: *You won't have sole responsibility, anyway, Wayne. I'll be moderating a sample of your marked assignments, and we'll also be doing some cross-moderation at the next section meeting. You've got the set of assessment criteria, haven't you?*

WAYNE: *Yes. Thanks. But what about giving feedback?*

HARRY: *Two important things to remember. First it's got to be constructive. In other words, don't just tell them what they've done wrong; tell them what they could do to make it better. And tell them what they've done well. There's always something to praise. And then the second thing is, it's got to be clear. They've got to be able to understand it. What you're aiming for is that they read your feedback and understand straightaway what they need to do next time to improve their work.*

WAYNE: *OK. So, how much should I write on their work?*

HARRY: *Keep it fairly brief. You don't want to be writing more than they have. Too much and they might be put off reading it. And I tend not to use a red pen. It's too much like school for some of them.*

WAYNE: *That's a shame. I was looking forward to the red pen ...*

Of course, assessment isn't confined to written assignments. Teachers in FE are assessing all the time: watching groupwork; taking question-and-answer sessions; observing learner performance in practical skills; keeping an eye on individuals' progress; and so on. Some of the suggestions Harry makes about written feedback apply equally to spoken feedback, particularly when it comes to issues of being clear and constructive.

Here is some useful assessment terminology to keep in mind.

» *Formative assessment*: assessment which the learner can use to improve future performance.

» *Summative assessment*: a final and definitive assessment, such as an exam at the end of a course.

» *Continuous assessment*: assessment which is ongoing throughout the course of study, in the form of assignments for example, which replace the need for an end exam.

» *Reliable assessment*: where the same assessment decision is reached regardless of who is the assessor. (The process of moderation is designed to ensure reliability.)

» *Valid assessment*: where the assessment task is appropriate and relevant to the skill or knowledge being assessed. (For example, a practical driving test is a valid assessment of a driver's skill, while a multi-choice theoretical test about how an internal combustion engine works is not.)

Further reading

To find out more about assessment in an FE context you could read:

Tummons, J. (2011) *Assessing Learning in the Lifelong Learning Sector* (2nd Edition). Exeter: Learning Matters.

A is for Authenticity

The principal of Bogginbrook College of FE is addressing staff at the start of the new academic year:

Colleagues, welcome. As I look around the team here, I can see quite a few different faces, and it's great to see new young staff coming in to replace some of the older experienced stagers we sadly had to say goodbye to last year.

I know we have embraced a lot of changes over the last year, and now, as we enter a new era in the development of Bogginbrook College of Further Education, we must build on these foundations to create a college fit for the twenty-first century. Here at Bogginbrook, we're all about creating added value for our students and the community at large. At the end of the day, it is our role to empower our learners, young and old, to contribute fully to UK PLC, and enable us to compete more effectively and efficiently in an increasingly globalised economy.

Continuous improvement in quality standards is what will enable us to deliver on the challenges we are being set by government, and this means evaluating our performance on an ongoing basis to ensure that we are providing real value for money. As we continue on this journey of change, our staff are the most valuable resource an organisation like ours has, so let us know your views. My senior colleagues and I have drawn up a vision and values statement for the college which we will be circulating shortly to seek your opinions. My door is always open ...

Any of this have a familiar smell about it? The truth is such talk may mask genuinely noble intentions, but research indicates that people are generally disinclined to believe what senior managers tell them, at the best of times. To suggest that, aside from our immediate boss, we are always on the lookout for a charlatan with a hidden agenda is therefore not cynical, but merely realistic.

Building and maintaining the trust of their team and their colleagues is not just crucial for senior managers but an essential part of good working relationships for every member of staff (see **T is for Trust**). And many writers on the subject highlight authenticity or integrity as a key component of trust. But what is authenticity, and where does it come from? Here are some thoughts.

> » It starts with self-awareness. Knowing yourself, being aware of your own strengths and shortcomings, and conscious of your emotional as well as intellectual responses helps you to be more sensitive to your impact on others. This is at the heart of emotional intelligence, which you can read more about in **E is for Emotional Intelligence**, and in Daniel Goleman's book, which you'll find in the Useful References.

» Awareness of your own learning needs goes hand in hand with asking for feedback, admitting your mistakes and knowing when to ask for help. Tough to do sometimes, because it can feel like weakness, but there is strong evidence that successful people, in all walks of life, are actually better at asking for help, because after all, this is how we learn.

» Understanding your own values enables you to acknowledge where these are compatible with those of the organisation and where they are not.

» Honesty and sincerity are obviously fundamental. Yet, you may not always feel that you can be entirely open with information. If so, then be straight about what you can and cannot discuss. Respecting confidences, after all, is also a marker of integrity and trustworthiness.

» Hands up if you've ever worked with a very plausible colleague who would say one thing to your face and then do another, intent on nothing so much as the advancement of their own career? If we are to behave authentically, we must do what we say we will do, and be seen to face up to bad news, whilst maintaining a positive focus on making things better.

» Some sort of ethical code to guide your decisions is vital when working in a rapidly changing environment, and often with incomplete information, as headline stories from the political and business world frequently remind us. Walter Bennis sees integrity as one of the four main competencies of leadership and talks about a 'moral compass' being the third leg of a tripod which leaders must keep in balance (Bennis and Thomas, 2002). The other two legs are ambition and competence. If any of these are too weak or too strong in relation to the others, then integrity is undermined.

B is for Behaviour Management

MADGE: *Help!*

ZOE: *What's up now, Madge?*

MADGE: *I've got the class from hell this afternoon.*

ZOE: *The* what? *You mean the level 2s? Who calls them that?*

MADGE: *Norman. You know. The head of school. He said they threatened to dangle the last trainee teacher out of the window.*

ZOE: *Oh for goodness ... Look, Madge, let's just say Norman has an unusual sense of humour, OK? That group is a bit noisy sometimes but they're basically a nice lot. What you have to remember is that 16- and 17-year-olds have a lot of energy and are easily bored. The trick is to plan your lesson carefully – give them clear goals; give them plenty to do; keep the pace up; give them a countdown to the end of each task and don't have them working on one activity for more than ten minutes.*

MADGE: *But what if they don't listen to me?*

ZOE: *Why wouldn't they listen to you? You're the teacher. Go in there; look confident; don't raise your voice; show them you've got a sense of humour ...*

Zoe makes it sound so easy. Managing learner behaviour is clearly not a problem for her. And the advice she's giving is sound enough. Careful and appropriate lesson planning combined with a show of confidence and humour are often enough to keep any class on track. But it's important to keep in mind a particular characteristic of the FE sector, which is that a significant number of its learners have not had a very positive experience of education up to the point where they enter college. They may have achieved less at school than they had hoped. They may have left school with a sense of failure. They may have had ambitions which they feel they can't now achieve, and FE may seem to them a second best option. All of these factors may have a negative impact on their motivation and behaviour. There's nothing the FE teacher can do to turn back the clock; but understanding the possible causes of difficult or non-compliant behaviour is one way in which you can forge a positive relationship with such learners and begin to rebuild their confidence and their self-esteem.

Here are some useful pointers to bear in mind if you encounter difficult behaviour in one of your classes.

» Don't take it personally. This is almost certainly not about you, but about the learner's previous experience or state of mind.

» Look at the behaviour as a message. What is it telling you? If the learner doesn't want to engage with the lesson is it perhaps because they're afraid of failing? Or of being laughed at by others in the class? Are they perhaps bored because it's too easy for them? Or are they desperate for your attention and will go to any lengths to get it? (In which case, find something to praise them for. If they discover they can get attention that way, everyone wins.)

» Don't be confrontational. This can cause a situation to escalate. It's much better, for example, to make a request rather than give an order. If you bark, *Sit down!* and the learner refuses, you are trapped in a battle of wills and the whole class will be watching with interest to see who wins. But if you say, *I would like you to sit down*, you are simply making a statement. If they don't comply, you can try again later, with as little fuss and fanfare as possible.

» If the problem behaviour isn't disrupting anyone else's learning, it's OK to pretend you haven't noticed it (yes, it really is) if addressing it would only draw the other learners' attention away from their task. Of course, some behaviours, such as dancing on a table, you can't feasibly pretend not to have noticed. But rather than put on a sideshow of teacher versus naughty student, a bit of strategic ignoring is sometimes the best option. And it has the added benefit of not rewarding the culprit's negative behaviour by paying attention to it.

» Always model the behaviour you expect of your students. If you want them to be enthusiastic about today's lesson, look enthusiastic yourself. If you want them to behave towards you and each other with a measure of respect, show them how it's done. And if you want them to turn up on time for class, always be punctual yourself.

(See also **R is for Respect.**)

Further reading

To find out more about motivating learners and managing difficult behaviour you could read:

Wallace, S. (2007) *Getting the Buggers Motivated in FE*. London: Continuum.

Wallace, S. (2013) *Managing Behaviour in FE* (3rd Edition). London: Sage/Learning Matters.

B is for Benchmarking

Picture this. Harry and Sheena have just come out of a Section Heads' meeting with the VP:

HARRY: *Psst! Sheena! What was he going on about? What does he mean, 'benchmarking'?*

SHEENA: *Benchmarking. You know what benchmarking means. It's when you compare where you are – in terms of standards – with where you want to be. It's about identifying what needs to be improved, looking around to see where it's done better – inside or outside the college – and then implementing those same strategies to make improvements. So basically it's about raising standards and improving quality. It's also been called the art of stealing shamelessly.*

HARRY: *But what's that got to do with benches, for goodness sake?*

SHEENA: *Oh, that's because of where the term comes from. It was originally about measuring productivity levels in industry. Management used to make a chalk mark on the work benches of those workers who were meeting the set targets, so other workers could follow their example.*

HARRY: *So if I arrive one morning and find the VP's chalked a big cross on my desk, I know I'm doing OK?*

SHEENA: *If that happened, Harry, I don't think it would be a good sign.*

Sheena has taken the *stealing shamelessly* quote from Owen (2002).

B is for Bullying

As an FE professional you have a three-fold responsibility with regard to the bullying of staff or students: how to spot it; how to stop it; and how to avoid doing it yourself or having it done to you.

How to spot bullying

Let's look first at how to spot it. Which of the following incidents, if any, would you say constitutes bullying as defined by your college's anti-bullying policy?

1. JASON: *Parveen, I need those retention and achievement figures right now.*
    PARVEEN: *I know. Sorry. They're not quite …*
    JASON: *You've had plenty of time to get them in. I need them now.*
    PARVEEN: *The trouble is, there's been so much paperwork …*
    JASON: *I don't want any more lame excuses. They told me you were useless when I first came here, and I can see they were right.*

2. NORMAN: *Evening.*
    ZOE: *Oh! Blimey, you scared me there. I thought I was the only one left in the building.*
    NORMAN: *I like to see my team working late. Now, I understand you've made a complaint to the VP about the recruitment of students in this school.*
    ZOE: *Er …*
    NORMAN: *I'm not quite sure why you went over my head, Zoe.*
    ZOE: *I didn't. I talked to you about it, and you said there was nothing you could do. And the thing is, Norman, we're recruiting kids onto the programme who just can't cope with the work. It's creating horrendous problems for the teaching team as well as for the learners …*
    NORMAN: *My advice to you, my dear, is don't rock the boat. It won't be good for your career prospects.*

3. SHEENA: *My desk is broken. Could I have a new one?*
    PARVEEN: *As head of school I have to say no.*
    SHEENA: *But everyone else has just had a new one.*
    PARVEEN: *Nothing left in the budget.*
    SHEENA: *Well, could I have a three-drawer filing cabinet? I've been struggling since I came here, storing everything in a couple of cardboard boxes. Everybody else has got a filing cabinet.*
    PARVEEN: *No. Nothing left in the budget.*

SHEENA:	*What about a key to the staff toilet? I still haven't got one. I'm the only one who hasn't.*
PARVEEN:	*No. Sorry. Budget.*
SHEENA:	*Couple of ballpoint pens?*
PARVEEN:	*No. Sorry.*

You are likely to find that your college's anti-bullying policy would identify all of these interactions as examples of bullying. In (1) Jason is perfectly within his rights as manager to chase Parveen for the R&A returns. Where he oversteps the mark is in his final remark where he insults and undermines her. Even if what he says is factually accurate here, his communicating it in this way and in this context constitutes bullying. In (2) it is not the fact that Norman confronts Zoe with what she has done, but rather that he lurks about after dark to catch her on her own and issues a veiled threat that defines this as bullying behaviour. In (3) the problem is not that Parveen says she can't afford to provide Sheena with necessary resources, but that she has managed to provide them for everyone else and is therefore discriminating against this one member of the school.

Bullying and harassment are often used interchangeably, with some organisations defining bullying as a form of harassment. Your college may have its own definition, but here is ours:

Harassment is any behaviour (such as statements or actions) which is based on any social factor and is offensive to any recipient. Social factor includes race, culture, nationality, ethnicity, religion, gender, sexuality, disability, age, marital status, physical trait or social status. Any recipient will include any person who witnesses the behaviour as well as the person to whom the behaviour is directed.

How to stop bullying

In terms of how to stop bullying, it is essential that college procedures are followed scrupulously. Failure to do so can compromise the fairness of the ensuing process as well as the legal position of the college and the individuals involved. As an employer, the college is responsible for preventing bullying and harassment, which can lead to low morale, stress, increased sickness absence, poor employee relations and the loss of talented people. It may also find itself taken to an employment tribunal answering claims of discrimination (see **I is for Inclusion**). You should therefore refer all alleged cases of staff bullying to the college's HR manager so that matters are investigated properly and correct procedures followed. It is rarely advisable for you to intervene, beyond an initial word with the parties involved to see whether a resolution can be reached informally before referring the matter on. Cases of alleged bullying should always be taken seriously; but unfortunately they are notoriously difficult to prove.

How to avoid bullying

As for the methods to avoid inadvertently being a bully yourself or being subjected to bullying, make sure you are familiar with your college's policy. As well as threats, insults and discrimination, bullying behaviour can include shouting, swearing, excluding or marginalising, spreading malicious rumours, ridiculing or demeaning, repeated unconstructive criticism or unwelcome sexual advances. Obviously all of these behaviours are not only to be avoided yourself but also treated with zero-tolerance within your team (see **Z is for Zero-Tolerance**).

Further reading

For more on bullying see the ACAS Website:

www.acas.org.uk/index.aspx?articleid=797.

C is for Challenging

Ever found yourself in a meeting, discussing a new initiative with colleagues, or talking to your boss about how she wants you to address a particular problem, and thought to yourself *This doesn't sound right to me. I'm sure I could suggest a better way ...?* Such situations tend to go one of three ways.

1. We decide to keep our mouths shut for fear of upsetting people, or being thought disruptive and awkward. Then kick ourselves afterwards when it all goes wrong or someone else points out the alternative we had in mind.

2. We get all self-righteous and fired up about how right we are and rubbish the prevailing idea, thus proving to everyone beyond doubt that we really are disruptive and awkward.

3. We manage to question the prevailing idea and introduce alternative thinking without undermining anyone or creating defensiveness.

So how do we set about ensuring that, when faced with these situations, we successfully go for the third option?

Some of the principles we describe in the section on feedback apply equally here. So, direct challenge carries the danger of being seen as a threat to other people's status and our perceived *intent* will affect how people respond. The more supportive we are, the more we position our views as intended to help the team/colleague/boss look good (as opposed to, say, showing off our superior intellect, seeking attention or getting revenge for a previous slight), then the more receptive others will be to our alternative ideas.

Let us look at some ways of doing this.

» ALTERNATIVE REALITIES – instead of framing our comments in terms of right and wrong (*no, that's wrong, what you need to do is....*), try setting them in the context of alternative realities or perspectives (*Well yes, that's certainly a valid way of looking at it, but an alternative view might be ...*).

» QUESTIONS NOT STATEMENTS – where statements can appear dogmatic and fixed, questions can be a gentler way of opening up different perspectives, without necessarily implying the other person is wrong (*Have you thought about what might happen if ...? How do you think students might respond to ...?*).

» DE-PERSONALISE – people feel more threatened and therefore more defensive if they think we are attacking them personally. So what about …

  — *I'm not sure that's the only assumption* RATHER THAN *No, you're wrong about that …*

  — *that response could be misinterpreted* RATHER THAN *They'll think you're a twit if you do that …*

  — *the overriding importance of hard measures may not be a value everyone shares* RATHER THAN *You're the only silly bugger obsessed with measuring everything that moves.*

» WONDERING – a useful and equally non-threatening variation on the questioning approach is to appear to be questioning oneself, or wondering (*I wonder if there's an alternative perspective here … I wonder what employers would think of this … I wonder what possessed anyone to promote you …*). Well, OK then, maybe not that last one!

» LISTEN, OBSERVE, VALIDATE, ENQUIRE (LOVE) – we can bring together many of the above principles in this routine for demonstrating supportive challenge. It reminds us to listen carefully to what is being proposed, demonstrate we have listened by making an observation, acknowledge the validity of the other person's view, and then offer our challenge in the form of a question (*Yes, OK Harry, you're arguing in favour of Wayne leading this project, as I understand it, because you think a newcomer will bring fresh ideas, and that's certainly a fair assumption. I wonder is there an alternative view here, which is that our project leader needs to be well-networked in the local community?*)

» WATCH YOUR 'BUT' – no, this is not a warning against back-stabbing colleagues. It is simply an observation that the word 'but' can act as a bit of a red rag to a bull when challenging others. It can undo a constructive challenge by making all that went before it seem like insincere flannel. In the example above we could have said *BUT I wonder is there an alternative …* It's a small point, but to the listener it may make the difference between coming across as contradiction or an attempt to *build* upon ideas.

Why are the skills of constructive challenge important to your college? Well, unless people are able to experiment with new ideas, challenge the status quo and engage in creative dialogue, without all this being seen as threatening, it is unlikely that goals around innovation and continuous improvement and learning will be fully met. And that means the competition will leave you behind …

C is for Change

Think back five years, or maybe just 12 months. How much has changed about your college, management structures, curriculum requirements, standards and targets, your job and what is expected of you? If the answer is not much, you probably don't work in further education and you've accidentally picked up the wrong book. Perhaps you've landed recently from outer space, or been defrosted from some glacier in the Dolomites, complete with flint axe and a slightly puzzled expression.

Organisations everywhere, inside and outside of the education sector, are experiencing continual change. The pace may vary, but the change never stops, and everyone has a part to play in helping their teams and their institutions respond successfully to what can sometimes seem like unmanageable chaos. (And sometimes it doesn't just *seem* that way ...)

Let's take just one small-scale example. At Bogginbrook College of Further Education, falling demand for programmes in secretarial and receptionist skills has led to the decision to merge the office arts section with the business studies section to create a School of Business. To examine the issues at stake, we will use a framework for change, which incorporates ideas from a number of eminent thinkers on the topic, including Barrett (1998), Bridges (1991), Kotter (1996), Schein (1992) and Senge (1990).

Now, have a look at this:

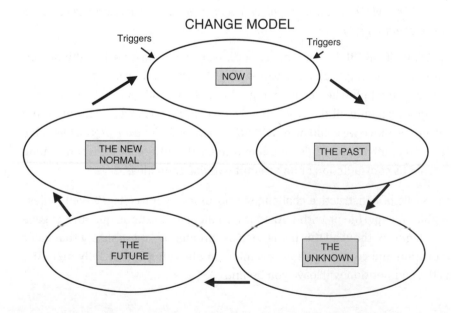

How can managers take account of each of these aspects of the change process in order to ensure that objectives are met and they bring people along with them as well?

Now

Change is usually the result of some combination of internal and/or external triggers. For example, a deterioration in our health or nagging from our friends or family may induce us to try to stop smoking. In the case of Bogginbrook College, falling student rolls have combined with financial pressures to raise questions about the viability of certain programmes and the departments which were built around them. Whatever the trigger, successful change generally starts with an understanding of where we are now and why.

This means listening to different accounts, or 'stories', in order to appreciate where different interest groups may be coming from, and what the strengths of the current state of affairs are, not just the weaknesses. Before rushing in to change anything, the senior managers at Bogginbrook must be sure that they have understood the reasoning behind the current departmental structure, what worked well about it, and how different groups of staff view the current challenge. They will then be better placed to anticipate the concerns of staff and the likely sources of resistance to change.

The past

Aside from failing to understand the present situation fully, one of the most common mistakes managers make when faced with change is to 'trash the past'. How often have you seen eager 'new brooms' come into an organisation (or indeed sector) only to criticise and sweep away all that has gone before, regardless of merit, in the cause of justifying their appointment?

If the Bogginbrook managers are shrewd, they will build a vision of what is over and done with and what is not, and communicate this clearly to staff, whilst at the same time showing respect for what has been achieved in the past. They will be unambiguous about what must change, but support people and help them to adjust their 'mental models' to cope with the new reality.

The unknown

If life were easy and change predictable and under our control, we would move seamlessly from old state to new state, just as we had planned it, with the grateful cheers of the college's staff ringing in our ears. Of course, what actually happens is we shove off from a safe and familiar harbour, expecting to discover the East Indies, and end up in an entirely new continent. Not only that, but in the meantime we have to cope with weeks or months of not knowing where the hell we are, or whether we will get anywhere at all.

Successful managers at every level prepare people for this uncertainty (even when they may be experiencing it themselves) and help them to cope with it by encouraging experimentation and new ideas. They accept the learning that failure brings. They use short-term action planning and review, so that people can see progress, however slight, and feel confident that change is happening. Most of all, they make themselves visible (see **W is for Walking Around**), and they over-communicate to ensure that no one feels isolated and consensus is reinforced.

The future

Let's imagine that at Bogginbrook the structural changes have now been achieved, roles have been changed and those whose jobs were lost have gone. The combined school is now in place and looks something like what was originally planned. As the future takes shape, the team leaders make a point of reminding people of that vision, the purpose behind the changes and what they were designed to achieve.

They also review success measures in order to celebrate early successes and try to prioritise actions, which will bring about 'quick wins'. In helping colleagues adjust to this new future, they do not exclusively focus on processes, systems and structures, but engage people in establishing the culture and values of the new school, appealing to hearts as well as minds by painting a compelling picture of all it will achieve.

The new normal

Anyone who has made a New Year's resolution understands the fragility of change and how good intentions slip back into old behaviours so easily when the pressure is on. Working in a new way once or twice does not guarantee permanent change.

For Bogginbrook to really embed the changes in its new school, it must continue to monitor performance and reinforce new approaches. It must ensure that knock-on effects to other schools and departments are managed, and policies and strategies altered where necessary to integrate the new structure. It must recognise the difference between grudging compliance and a genuine behaviour change, which stems from new learning and a shift in underlying assumptions about the way things should work.

Ultimately, change will only truly be embedded when people don't just do things differently, but feel and think differently too. It is an emotional journey for each individual, as well as a rational one, with all of the uncertainties and unpredictability that that implies. Understanding this is a good start to recognising what managers and team leaders can and cannot control, and accepting that, to be successful and lasting, change must gain acceptance and not simply be imposed.

Here's that diagram again, this time summarising the key factors that come into play when we engage in institutional change.

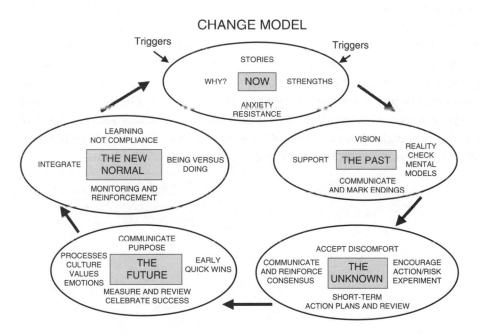

CHANGE MODEL

C is for the Cinderella Sector

Ever wondered where this over-used metaphor came from? Well, it was Kenneth Baker, in his role as Secretary of State for Education under Margaret Thatcher back in the 1980s, who described FE as a Cinderella – always undervalued and under-funded. This seemed to hold out a promise of better times to come, of course, when Cinderella would actually get to go to the ball. It also, rather bizarrely, appeared to cast schools and higher education in the role of ugly sisters; although – strange to say – you'll rarely hear either of them referred to as the Ugly Sister sector.

So what does this suggest for your role, as an FE professional? Are you Buttons, or the Fairy Godmother, or the Handsome Prince? Gender aside, you'll probably find yourself, at one time or another, enacting all of these. As Buttons you can be the sympathetic colleague, who can empathise and sympathise, have a chat, have a joke, be approachable. As the Fairy Godmother you can act as mentor, or make things happen, or put things right. The problematic side of this role, of course, is that you may be expected to solve every problem with a wave of your wand. You may even have that expectation of yourself, which is just asking for trouble. As the Handsome Prince you may find yourself in a position to promote and demote (though hopefully not on the basis of people's shoe size). You will certainly find yourself in a high profile position where your decisions and conduct have the potential to win or lose you the respect of those you work with. Above all, you will be in a position to do something – however small – to enhance the reputation of FE and raise its profile and its status.

C is for Coaching

Which would you prefer: a coach or a mentor?

What makes you say that?

The chances are your response may depend on a number of things.

- » What stage in your career you are at.
- » Whether you have ever experienced a 'learning partnership' of this sort and what you called it.
- » A host of associations these terms have acquired for you by dint of how you have heard them used in your particular experience.

So, unsurprisingly, the question often results in an interesting range of replies:

I've been teaching for ten years. I'd be mortified if the college offered me the services of a mentor ... Nobody's telling me how to do my job ...

The thing about a coach is they let you find your own solutions ...

Coaches tell you how you can improve at what you do ...

I think a mentor is what I need; someone who will just listen to what I am struggling with and let me find my own solutions ...

Yes, I'd definitely prefer a coach. Isn't that what executives have? ...

The quality of coaching and mentoring within colleges is coming under increasing scrutiny during inspections and self-assessment exercises. But the truth is mentoring has been a well-recognised term in the education sector for some time, and has tended to get used for a very wide range of interventions. People's understanding is influenced by long-established models, such as older students mentoring younger ones, and, more recently, the concept of 'learning mentors'. Coaching, on the other hand, is a much more recent term, other than on the sports field, and its growing currency, inside and outside education, leads to a certain amount of confusion about how it is different from mentoring, if at all.

Maybe we should approach this from a different angle?

Both mentoring and coaching consist of a conversation or series of conversations, which help a person to learn, change or come to decisions in a way that enables them to achieve their objectives or get better at what they do. The principle behind both, as with much adult learning, is that people are more motivated to learn when they are helped to find their own answers, and encouraged to reflect on their experiences, good and bad, in order to gain insights which help them to improve. These 'learning conversations' share much the same set of helpful activities. Among many others these include:

- » listening;
- » questioning;
- » challenging;
- » supporting;
- » encouraging;
- » creating insight through reflection;
- » providing feedback;
- » summarising;
- » raising awareness;
- » generating options;
- » identifying priorities;
- » building confidence;
- » sharing knowledge and experience;
- » acting as sounding board;
- » being a critical friend;
- » action planning;
- » unlocking potential and latent know-how.

So, in a way, these two processes have a lot more in common than they have differences. In fact, if you were observing one of these 'learning conversations' with any or all of the above activities going on, it is unlikely that you would be able to accurately determine whether you were watching coaching or mentoring.

So why don't we call them both the same thing? Well, it's true that would put a stop to endless and largely fruitless debates on training courses. But the truth is, despite all the crossover, and the increasingly interchangeable way these terms are being used, there are still some characteristics which distinguish the majority of coaching relationships from the majority of mentoring relationships. More coaching relationships than not tend to be:

» focused more on skills, knowledge and behaviours;

» performance-orientated;

» following a shared agenda.

More mentoring relationships than not tend to be:

» focused on longer-term transitions;

» dealing with future personal and career growth;

» following the learner's agenda.

We say 'more than not' deliberately. Because there are hundreds of exceptions to even these tentative distinctions. But let us see how they might clear up some of the confusion in our sector. What name would you give the following examples?

1. You are an experienced lecturer or section leader who has been observing a newly qualified lecturer give a lesson and are now taking her through your feedback.

2. You are a head of department who has been approached by a section leader you know from another school wanting to think about whether they should stay in FE or move back into industry.

3. A colleague has approached you about problems he is having with classroom discipline. You are both two or three years into the profession, but you've always been better at that sort of thing.

4. Some project experience running a new course design team has made you wonder whether you would enjoy more of a management role in future. Who could you approach to help you think about this, and what would you call them?

(Answers at the end of this section.)

So who might get involved in coaching you? Well, the college may have invested in training a specific set of people to undertake this, in order, for example, to provide specialist subject support in teaching standards. These will usually be experienced lecturers and whilst their prime focus will be on trainees and newly qualified staff, they may also be asked to help experienced staff improve their performance in a particular area, maybe as a result of performance review or appraisal outcomes or at their own request.

Alternatively, it may be your immediate manager who provides coaching, formally or informally, as part of their responsibility for your performance and your continuing professional development. This might be focused on teaching skills or on other aspects of your role, such as management.

Both of these coaches will be helping you to achieve standards, guidelines and competencies laid down by government and the college in which you work. This is what we mean when we say the agenda is SHARED.

But you may also engage in peer coaching with a colleague, where you identify complementary skills and the potential to learn from each other. Here the agenda may be more informal, but will still probably be influenced partly by the recognised professional standards.

Whatever form the coaching takes, it should be undertaken by someone trained in the necessary skills (see also **L is for Listening, F is for Feedback, I is for Interviews**), and the conversation should be structured in such a way as to produce some learning outcome. There are many process models in the coaching literature, but most follow the stages enshrined in the Kolb learning cycle. In other words, they require an examination of an experience, reflection on that experience, drawing lessons or conclusions from our reflection, and finally changing our behaviour as a result. Incidentally, you will no longer be surprised to hear that mentoring conversations follow a very similar pattern.

> » ENGAGING – it helps to first agree a few ground rules concerning meetings, confidentiality, how the coaching fits with other processes and relationships, and what you each need to do to ensure the coaching is effective. Most importantly, it helps to agree what outcome the coaching is intended to achieve. This is not a one-off task. Ground rules and learning goals both change with time. However, as an individual coach/manager, or as a college, you may have some standard parameters that need to be laid down.

> » EXAMINING EXPERIENCE AND IDENTIFYING OPPORTUNITIES – this involves reviewing a person's experiences, identifying strengths, understanding where they may have struggled, and helping them to formulate an action plan incorporating the necessary national or institutional standards, or, where appropriate, to devise their own clear and measurable objectives for learning, change and improvement. This is where feedback from classroom observation comes in.

> » GENERATING OPTIONS AND IDEAS – you may then want to think through different options, new techniques or ideas, and reflect on how effective

these could be in helping achieve your objectives. The emphasis here is on keeping an open mind and exploring 'what ifs'.

» COMMITMENT TO ACTION – all this effort is wasted unless it results in some action, which of course leads to more learning. This will require weighing up pros and cons, thinking about priorities for learning and considering what is practical and achievable, given the resources available. So the aim of any coaching conversation, and every series of conversations, is to agree SMART objectives (see **O is for Objectives**), which will result in the coachee actually doing something. This can then be monitored and reflected upon at subsequent meetings.

A final word: please remember that coaching is not always the most appropriate form of learning or leadership. When your driving instructor sees you heading into the path of an oncoming lorry, he is unlikely to ask you a good question (unless it's *What the **** do you think you're doing?!!*). Sometimes we need to be told what to do (see **C is for Consult or Control).** But knowing when to help people learn for themselves is the mark of a good teacher and a good manager.

Answers

How did you do on our little quiz earlier? Well, according to our typology, numbers 1 and 3 look like coaching, and 2 and 4 look more like a mentoring relationship.

C is for Conflict

Norman, head of school for travel and tourism, has invited his three team leaders to a meeting to try and address an unseemly row that has broken out over car parking.

NORMAN: *Thanks for coming guys. Now, I believe there has been some misunderstanding between you about who's entitled to what parking space, or something ...*

ANGELA: *No, Norman, it's not a misunderstanding. It's just that Raj is such an arrogant p***k that he thinks he can plonk his crappy little Datsun wherever he likes, while everyone else has to abide by the agreed rules.*

RAJ: *You mean the informal, not-written-down-anywhere, donkey's-years-old, made-up-by-Angela rules? Is it those rules you're referring to?*

NORMAN: *Now, calm down, calm down, you two. I'm sure we can sort this out. Surely, if there's already an arrangement, Raj, even an informal one, the easiest thing is just to abide by this, isn't it?*

RAJ: *No one follows those daft rules anymore. The fact is that Angela here is whining about some grandmother rights she thinks she should keep, when we've had a fair lottery draw and I got the one space right outside the building, while she has to park further away.*

NORMAN: *Ah well, if that's the case, you know, there's been a draw, Angela, then maybe Raj is right. I mean fair's fair and all that ...*

ANGELA: *What?! You cannot be serious? Who said we were suddenly going to start having a lottery? I certainly didn't. Now as a vulnerable woman, I have to walk across campus in the dark, while I-run-marathons Raj here parks right outside the bloody offices.*

RAJ: *Oh come off it! Please don't play the vulnerable woman card. The campus is lit up like Diwali, and who the hell is going to ravish you?*

NORMAN: *No, now come on. This is getting personal ... Why don't you just agree to share the parking space ... Maybe a day or week each?*

ZOE: *Might I ask a question, Norman? What has changed to create this situation?*

NORMAN: *Hang on Zoe, don't interrupt. I think I might be onto something here ...*

ANGELA: *There's absolutely no way I'm sharing, and what has changed, for your information, is that the college is introducing parking fees for everyone below head of school, unless there is a so-called custom and practice arrangement in place. So Raj here suddenly gets the bright idea that the whole school should have a lottery ...*

ZOE: *So what exactly are you each wanting?*

ANGELA/RAJ: *Free parking, duh!*

ZOE: *And the rest of the staff in this building?*

ANGELA: *Well, I suppose, you know ... those who drive to work at least ...*

NORMAN: *Wait a minute! You mean I get a free parking space even though I come to work by train?*

This may not be the most important topic on the college agenda (well, maybe for some), but it is typical of the kind of thing which gets people all wound up and ready to do battle. The way we handle conflict at work has a huge effect on our productivity, our morale, our sense of teamwork and our job satisfaction. No one wants to work in a toxic environment, and yet we so often deal with conflict in a way which perpetuates that kind of atmosphere, rather than preventing it.

The first thing to say is that we cannot banish conflict altogether, and nor would we want to. The kind of interpersonal conflict Norman is trying (and failing) to deal with above is more often than not destructive, and managing people in such a way as to minimise it makes sense. But what about conflict around the way processes work or tasks are performed? Remove this and you have a workplace in which ideas and opinions are never questioned, new ways of doing things do not see the light of day, and all innovation and improvement is effectively strangled at birth.

So we all need to have the skills to manage conflict productively and professionally. How do our fictional staff cope do you think?

Well Norman, as the boss, is at least attempting to address the situation. He could have taken the line of least resistance and ignored the furore, so we should at least salute him for that. But look at what he does. Norman is desperately going for a quick compromise, to get all this unpleasantness out of the way as soon as possible. He swings wildly between favouring Angela or Raj, depending on whose argument he's just heard. His big idea is to cut the baby in half. We often assume that compromise is the best solution to conflict, whereas ideally we should be searching for an outcome that satisfies the needs of all parties. Norman makes no serious attempt to explore the facts dispassionately or to find out what each party really wants. In the end, this is left to Zoe, and whilst we don't know what the final outcome is, at least the slanging match has been replaced by a more measured examination of the problem.

Pedler *et al.* (2007) identified a number of different conflict resolution styles, which are determined by a combination of assertiveness and co-operativeness. These are summarised in the table below:

	UNCOOPERATIVE		CO-OPERATIVE
HIGHLY ASSERTIVE	COMPETING		COLLABORATING
		COMPROMISING	
UNASSERTIVE	AVOIDING		ACCOMMODATING

Norman's style veers between accommodating and compromising, and as for Raj and Angela, well they are stuck in competing mode. Only Zoe is exploring the possibility of collaboration. She is asking questions and trying to understand, without favouring any one point of view. Part of our problem in handling conflict may be cultural. Many of our institutions, such as law courts, parliament, and even education, are predicated on a model of debate. In other words, two sides take a fixed point of view and try to convince the other side that they are right. More often than not, this results in entrenching existing views and increasing resistance to change (just listen to *Today in Parliament*). A step up from this, argues David Clutterbuck (2007), we could call discussion. In this approach each party has something they want to achieve, but is willing to listen and accept some of the other party's views. (Many attempts at *consultation* feel a bit like this, at best.) The end result is usually minor changes and some sort of compromise. But arguably the most constructive way of handling conflict is dialogue, defined as addressing an issue with as open a mind as possible, trying to really understand the other person's perspective and perhaps creating a new perspective. This is the only mindset that leads to commitment and willingness to change on both sides.

So what might this kind of approach look like in practice? Well, take a look at the behaviours below and compare them to what you see happening in our example at the beginning of this section.

>> Establish common ground at the start.

>> Separate personalities from the real problem.

>> Encourage 'constructive conflict'.

>> Explore feelings as well as facts. But above all ask QUESTIONS.

>> Establish people's needs, rather than dwelling on negotiating positions.

>> Gain acceptance that disagreements are a group responsibility.

>> Encourage joint problem-solving.

>> Bear in mind that you may need to adjust your own view.

(Adapted from Bolman and Deal, 1991, and West, 1994)

C is for Consult or Control

This section briefly addresses one key aspect of team leadership, which is the question of 'command and control' versus more consultative and involving styles. What is the right amount of freedom to give people, in order to motivate and develop them? Does control make for efficient management and higher quality standards, or does it merely stifle creativity and erode the initiative and energy of your best people? Some sections in this book (see **C is for Change**, **C is for Coaching**, **D is for Delegation**, **M is for Mentoring**) may seem to favour freedom, whilst others (**D is for Disciplinary**, **M is for Meetings**, **O is for Objectives**) contain more elements of control and standardisation.

You may feel that there is a place for both control and individual initiative, and indeed, effective leaders tend to find their own balance between these extremes. They adjust this balance depending on the circumstances and the individual person they are dealing with. This contingency approach has been written about by various people, but perhaps made most accessible by Ken Blanchard (Blanchard, 1986), he of the *One Minute Manager* books. You can find references in our suggested reading.

In his model, the leadership approach is defined by the degree of direction given (high or low) and the degree of support given (high or low). This gives four broad categories, or leadership styles, which the leader may move between according to the demands of the situation and the individual.

» DIRECTIVE – high degree of direction, but low support. In other words, the leader gives detailed instructions, which are not for debate, and expects them to be followed.

» COACHING – high degree of direction and lots of support too. So the leader still tells people the task and the way to do it, but also offers to help and coach the person in achieving it. (Do not confuse this convenient label with coaching itself, which may, like leadership, be more or less directive.)

» SUPPORTING – low levels of direction, but highly supportive. Here, the leader trusts the person's ability to achieve the task with little direction as to how, but they are ready to jump in and provide additional help if problems of commitment or motivation arise.

» DELEGATING – low in both direction and support. The leader places enough confidence in someone's experience and reliability to simply 'agree and forget'. Given a clear objective, they are confident the person will deliver without any interference from them.

Having established this outline, we can probably all think of times in our lives when we've been on the receiving end of each of these styles of leadership, and no doubt we will recall some of them more fondly than others, depending on how appropriately they were used. Try matching the following examples to what you think is the appropriate style.

1. *Sheena has many years' experience at the college and knows the local area well. She is actually very capable, but her confidence has taken a hammering, due to a history of bullying by overbearing bosses. You want her to take on liaison with secondary schools in your vicinity.*

2. *Zoe, a bright and enthusiastic new member of staff, has just joined your faculty from another college, and this is her first leadership role. You are helping her to organise her first major field trip for students.*

3. *Kimberley, the highly efficient school secretary, has worked at the college just about longer than any other member of staff. She is renowned for her annual organisation of the staff barbecue, which has developed over the years into quite an event. You want her to sort out this year's do.*

4. *Harry is relatively new to the role of section leader, and you suspect he may have been over-promoted. He does not always make a priority of what he sees as extra-curricular tasks and struggles to keep up to speed with the rapidly-changing FE environment. You think a change of scene might help test his mettle, and arrange for him to lead a new adult numeracy programme, something he has not done before.*

What's your view? Here's ours:

Sheena will probably require Supporting, since she knows what needs to be done, it is just a question of the confidence to do it. Zoe is highly motivated, but inexperienced and unfamiliar with her new environment. The safety risk is high, so it is best to adopt a Directive style at first. Kimberley clearly knows what she is doing and relishes her task. A Delegating style should be safe to use here. Finally, Harry is not only unfamiliar with his new task, but may be inclined to give it a low priority. He will probably need the high direction and support of a Coaching approach.

In reality, of course, there are many more subtleties of leadership style than our simple summary would suggest. Assuming there is always one right answer may be seen as somewhat naïve. But this kind of model at least encourages us to be flexible and consider the needs of the individual team member, as well as helping us to think about how we might employ different approaches in different circumstances.

C is for Critical Thinking

Thinking skills are now part of the school curriculum, and so most school-leavers who enter FE will have experience of this (although in some it may not always be apparent). Thinking skills, as a subject, usually involves problem-solving and classroom discussion, and is seen as means of developing *cognitive acceleration*, especially in the sciences. It may include *lateral thinking* exercises, such as those devised by Edward de Bono (b.1933); or an approach known as *philosophy for children*, developed by the American, Matthew Lipman (b.1922), where ideas and anomalies are explored through the discussion of stories. But what do we mean by *critical* thinking? Sarah explains to Raj and Zoe:

SARAH: *You're both going to be teaching on HE courses next term. Most of the learners will have come up through the FE route. They'll be hardworking and motivated. They'll have good cognitive skills. And one of the things you'll be doing with them is to help them develop their critical thinking skills. This is about encouraging them to think not just about what, but also about how and why. It's about being analytical, and questioning things, and looking for the possible flaws in an argument or theory.*

RAJ: *That's quite difficult, isn't it? Because up to this point most of them have experienced a curriculum where things are either right or wrong. A right way of doing things and a wrong way. Competent or not competent. They've not really been required or encouraged to question things.*

SARAH: *That's right.*

ZOE: *So that's going to have an impact on the way we teach, isn't it? Much more discussion, I guess. And more in-depth questioning.*

RAJ: *And building up their confidence to think critically. That's going to be the big thing.*

ZOE: *I'm really looking forward to it.*

Critical thinking, then, is really a set of skills: the ability to analyse an argument and find its strengths and weaknesses; the ability to distinguish fact from opinion and to ask questions about 'why' and 'how' rather than simply accumulate facts. It's about having the confidence and curiosity to ask questions, weigh up alternatives, and solve problems. The largely competence-based curriculum of much FE provision does not appear on the face of it, as Raj points out, to place much emphasis on this critical and questioning approach. But critical thinking is an essential skill for practitioners and managers working within the sector, and certainly becomes an important component of higher level and professional qualifications.

Further reading

Cottrell, S. (2011) *Critical Thinking Skills*. Abingdon: Routledge.

C is for Curriculum

We get the word curriculum from the Latin, meaning a race track around which people run for the amusement of others. An apt description of the teacher's role, you might think. And we use it in several senses: there's the 'big' curriculum, by which we refer to all the provision the college offers, and there's the 'little' curriculum, by which we refer to the course content and processes of the particular course we're teaching on. There's also the *vocational curriculum* in general, about which there is much lively and ongoing debate. Some, like Richard Pring (1999) argue that the vocational curriculum as it currently exists in England and Wales is too instrumental, insufficiently inspiring, and should be broadened to encompass a wider and more general range of subjects, such as thinking skills or a foreign language (see also **E is for Employability Skills**). On the other side of the debate are those who argue that the vocational curriculum should be designed specifically around the skills that employers want, and that our current competence-based curriculum serves this purpose very well.

Further reading

For a discussion of the advantages of a broader, more liberal curriculum for vocational education and training you could read:

Pring, R. (1999) *Closing the Gap: Liberal Education and Vocational Preparation*. London: Hodder & Stoughton.

D is for Delegation

Delegation is a term which is bandied about more often than it is understood.

When a manager delegates, they should be giving someone else the **authority**, responsibility and **initiative** to perform some **agreed** task. The key words here are the ones in bold, because they are usually the first ones to be forgotten by poor delegators. What they do is try to dump all the responsibility onto you, whether you want it or not, and give you no additional authority or help. This is just abdication. Worse still, is when they do this and then constantly stick their nose in and interfere, because *you're not doing it right.*

Good delegation implies that the manager retains some overall control, and checks on the performance of their team member. It also implies that both parties are willing for this responsibility to be re-assigned.

Of course, if it all goes pear-shaped, the manager cannot escape responsibility, even though she has delegated the task. It is her fault because she has delegated badly. It's tough at the top.

Having said that, delegation brings all sorts of benefits.

> » It helps you improve your use of time.
>
> » It makes the team more flexible by encouraging shared tasks and know-how.
>
> » It motivates your team.
>
> » It helps to grow and develop your team members.
>
> » It therefore leads to more potential successors.

So what stops leaders and managers from delegating properly?

1. It leads to more potential successors.
2. They're frightened of losing control.
3. The team member is not properly trained to carry out the task.
4. They like to stick with old jobs they know they're good at.
5. They tend to think only they can do the job 'properly' (ie in the same way).

6.   The task is not really suitable, perhaps for confidentiality reasons.

7.   They cannot be bothered to explain a task to someone else.

8.   It makes them feel secure to do something the team can't.

9.   The task is too urgent for them to have time to brief someone else properly.

If you are thinking that some of these reasons sound better than others, you are right. Which do you think are the acceptable reasons not to delegate? (See our view at the end of this section.)

Nevertheless, by following a few simple guidelines, effective delegation can be within every professional's grasp.

» Ensure you fully understand the purpose and contribution of *your* job.

» Identify *your* priority objectives and how your team can contribute to these.

» Think which tasks may be suited to delegation.

» Ensure you understand the strengths, future potential, and current workload of each of your team. Do not put individuals under undue stress.

» Decide what should be delegated, who can handle it and benefit from it, and whether any additional training is needed.

» Agree SMART objectives, including precise timescales, and ensure limits of authority are understood (see **O is for Objectives**).

» Agree how performance will be monitored.

» Make sure other relevant people know what you've done.

» Allow the team member to take the initiative, but be available to help.

» Give constructive feedback and allow people to take the credit.

And if you are not a manager? How do you avoid being dumped on by someone who wouldn't know good delegation if they fell over it? Well, you simply try a little upwards coaching and ensure your boss follows the above list. Make sure you agree SMART objectives and how performance will be monitored, check that other people have been properly communicated with, be sure to request help when you need it, and if you're not receiving feedback, then ask.

Will things go wrong occasionally? Will people let you down? Well yes, obviously. Delegation will always be a calculated risk. But bear in mind that there is nothing that reflects better on a manager than growing a team of able people and potential successors, who continually get the chance to impress others with what they can do.

(We would only see 3, 6 and 9 as valid reasons not to delegate.)

D is for Disciplinary

A number of complaints have been made over the last year against Angela. She has taught at Bogginbrook College for 28 years. She's a section leader in Norman's school, and the start of the complaints has coincided with her being given responsibility – against her express wishes – for co-ordinating the 14–16 provision within the school. This role carries no enhancement in terms of salary or promotion. The complaints are as follows.

» She's been consistently late for her classes and has, on seven occasions, not turned up for a scheduled class at all. (Source of complaint: students.)

» She's been absent from college on two occasions for over a week without notifying Norman, her manager, or making arrangements for her classes or management duties to be covered. (Source of complaint: Norman, her head of school.)

» She has completed no attendance registers – neither hard copy nor electronic – for three terms, nor completed last term's retention and achievement returns. (Source of complaint: Norman, her head of school.)

» She has spoken disparagingly about – and directly to – the 14–16 year old students, referring to them as *Babbies*, *No-hopers* and *Losers*. (Source of complaint: parents and students.)

» The achievement and retention figures for her section are very poor and two recent college self-assessment reports found her teaching to be 'unsatisfactory'.

This is what her head of school, Norman, has to say:

Angela doesn't seem willing to address any of these issues, and is particularly defensive about her teaching being criticised. And I'm not happy about her response to the paperwork issues and her unauthorised absence. I've told her I'm not satisfied, and I've arranged a meeting for next Wednesday so I can let her know what the next steps will be.

Now, whatever we may think of Norman and his management style, we need to look at this case dispassionately in order to judge whether disciplinary action is appropriate. Disciplinary action may be taken against a member of staff for a range of reasons. There may have been misconduct of some kind, or the member of staff's performance may be in question. In Angela's case it seems to be a matter of both. If the complaints had only concerned her performance in teaching and supporting learning, the first resort could have been to employ informal methods (such as CPD, or **Mentoring and Coaching**) to improve her performance. If this proved ineffective, only then would disciplinary action become inevitable. And of course it's essential to remember that the purpose of disciplinary action, too, is to improve performance. But we must also bear in mind that the final sanction for management – if no improvement is evident – is the power to dismiss.

In case you should need to instigate, or should become caught up in, a disciplinary process, you will need to make yourself familiar – if you are not already – with your College Disciplinary Policy and Procedure. It's also important that you understand and bear in mind the constraints under which the college management operates and particularly the broad legal framework which protects an employee against unfair or constructive dismissal. ACAS emphasise the following principles in their code of practice.

> » Employers and employees should act **consistently**.

> » Employers should carry out any necessary **investigations,** to establish the facts of the case.

> » Employers should **inform** employees of the basis of the problem and give them an opportunity to **put their case** in response before any decisions are made.

> » Employers should allow employees to be **accompanied** at any formal disciplinary meeting.

> » Employers should allow an employee to **appeal** against any formal decision made.

Your own college policy will include this and more, but you can also find helpful advice on the ACAS Website (accessed June 28, 2013):

www.acas.org.uk/media/pdf/k/b/Acas_Code_of_Practice_1_on_disciplinary_and_grievance_procedures-accessible-version-Jul-2012.pdf.

Further reading

Chapter 13 of the following covers issues of discipline and dismissal:

Torrington, D. *et al.* (2001) *Human Resource Management.* London: Prentice Hall.

D is for Diversity

One of the most interesting and challenging aspects of working in the FE sector is the sheer range and diversity of its learners. They are diverse in terms of age, prior achievement, aspirations, ability and expectations in a way that learners in the other two sectors – schools and universities – usually are not. Meeting the needs of a diverse range of learners is primarily about ensuring equality of access and opportunity regardless of gender, age, ethnicity, religion, sexual orientation, disability and so on (see **I is for Inclusion**). FE has only recently emerged from a culture of gender-specific expectations, where skills areas such as construction were taught by, and recruited, males, while areas such as caring targeted their recruitment specifically at female learners. The current culture of diversity is evident now (or certainly should be) in promotional material and college Website pages where illustrations represent a diverse range of learners rather than appearing to target specific, single sex or mono-cultural groups.

For the FE teacher, supporting diversity means encouraging a culture of tolerance and understanding, and taking measures to ensure that no learner feels excluded because of 'difference'. One of the most common issues for teachers is the question of how diverse learning needs can be met within a single lesson. One of the ways this is addressed is through differentiation. Learners may be given differentiated tasks according to their needs and level of achievement. Teachers may also introduce differentiated assessment, where learners who are achieving well are assessed on a wider range or higher level of outcomes than those who need more time and support.

Further reading

For a useful examination of diversity issues you could read:

Peart, S. (2012) *Making Education Work: How Black Men and Boys Navigate the Further Education Sector*. London: Trentham.

E is for Emotional Intelligence

Where your own Christmas e-mail to your section might say:

Thanks to all of you for all your hard work this term. I hope those of you who are able to spare the time will join me in room 001 for mince pies and cheese this lunchtime.

Norman's might read:

I remind colleagues that the College does not officially finish until 5pm this evening. CCTV cameras in the car park will record anyone leaving early.

This may be because Norman is not very emotionally intelligent.

It has become quite fashionable to talk about different intelligences. And, however you define them, it's likely that, as a professional in FE, you've found you're going to need every single one of them. Emotional intelligence is a term popularised by Goleman (1996). It means, among very many other things, the ability to read how others are feeling; the ability to imagine yourself in someone else's shoes. The intelligence to speak and act in a way that takes account of how others may be feeling is clearly a useful (though arguably not yet sufficiently widespread) skill. An emotionally intelligent teacher or manager will typically be one who builds up people's self-esteem, treats them with respect, consults (where possible) rather than dictates. They should never be confused with a 'soft' or non-assertive teacher or manager. Indeed, they may have a quite directive style. But what their emotional intelligence will provide above all is the ability to build and motivate effective learners and teams.

How is this achieved? It begins with being aware of your own emotions and how they may impact upon your judgement or behaviour at any given time. This aspect of emotional intelligence is too often overlooked, a too common assumption being that to demonstrate emotional intelligence we have to be warm and cuddly or do a lot of crying in public. This isn't at all what emotional intelligence is about. Developing a greater awareness of your own emotional responses to people and situations enables you to take a step back and reflect before you act. Is your colleague Norman really a poor manager, for example, or is it just that you find his style antithetical and irritating? Is Angela's performance really giving cause for concern, or is your unease about her partly because she reminds you of your Auntie Joan who scared the pants off you? Does that learner set out to annoy you, or is it that her behaviour reminds you of someone who used to bully you at school?

Emotional intelligence, then, is about recognising and addressing the fact that your own emotions may influence your attitudes and behaviour; and at the same time recognising the emotional impact your behaviour may have on others.

For the record, you're probably right to be concerned about Norman (see **B is for Bullying**) and Angela (see **D is for Disciplinary**), though it's to be hoped that someone with sufficient emotional intelligence further up the line of management might spot a link between the two sets of behaviours and treat it as a wider management problem.

E is for Employability Skills

Parveen is Harry's line manager. She corners him in the corridor.

PARVEEN: *Oh, Harry. A word.*

HARRY: *Just on my way to a class. In a bit of a hurry.*

PARVEEN: *Never mind that. I understand from one of your level 3 groups that you've been spending lesson time discussing television programmes with them. You really can't afford to be wasting time like that, you know. There's so much to get through ...*

HARRY: *Oh!* The Apprentice. *I was discussing* The Apprentice *with them. Well, not discussing exactly. I used it as an example. We were talking about entrepreneurship.*

PARVEEN: *No time for that, Harry. No time to chat about television.*

HARRY: *I just mentioned it, that's all. It occupied about 20 seconds of the lesson ...*

PARVEEN: *Your job is to turn out competent people for the workforce. That's what employers want. Not people who chat about television. Teach them, test them, stick to the unit specifications. That's all. Bye.*

The employability of its learners is one of the indicators by which an FE college judges its success; and this, of course, may go some way towards explaining Parveen's expressions of concern. Enabling people to succeed in the job market is the sector's prime directive, confirmed by the Foster report of 2005 which defined the role of the FE sector as one of skills training (see **F is for Foster Report**). To this end, the design and content of the competence-based qualification system is informed by the requirements of employers. Some critics have argued that this is too instrumental an approach and that we would be better served by a vocational curriculum which included some elements of a liberal or general education, as is the case in countries with stronger economies such as Germany (see **C is for Curriculum**). Richard Pring, for example, argues that:

there seems no reason why the liberal should not be conceived as something vocationally useful and why the vocationally useful should not be taught in an educational and liberating way. (Pring, 1999, p 183)

Parveen clearly doesn't share this view. But in any case Harry's use of an example that will be familiar to all his learners seems entirely reasonable to us, and in no way heralds the encroachment of a liberal curriculum to threaten the centrality of the employability agenda.

Further reading

To find out more about the argument for a broader curriculum in FE you could read:

Pring, R. (1999) *Closing the Gap: Liberal Education and Vocational Preparation*. London: Hodder & Stoughton.

Gravells, A. (2010) *Delivering Employability Skills in the Lifelong Learning Sector*. Exeter: Learning Matters.

E is for Engagement 1

No, this isn't about diamond rings or dates in the diary. It's about learners showing an interest in their learning. FE teachers sometimes encounter learners who seem unwilling or unable to engage with lessons. We touched on some of the reasons for this under **B is for Behaviour Management**. But what can be done to encourage engagement? Harry has a few suggestions for Wayne.

HARRY: *I know the group you're talking about, mate. They can be hard work.*

WAYNE: *I'm starting to wonder what they're doing on the course when they're showing so little interest in it.*

HARRY: *Well, they're easily bored, aren't they? It's their age, partly. They're only just out of school. Here's a checklist of things to try. Start with yourself. Do you look interested and enthusiastic?*

WAYNE: *Yes. Check. But getting less so, I have to tell you.*

HARRY: *Are you giving them interesting things to do?*

WAYNE: *Yes. Check. Well, I think they're interesting.*

HARRY: *Hmm. Are you injecting a bit of competition into the tasks you give them? Playing team against team – that sort of thing?*

WAYNE: *No. But good idea. I'll try that.*

HARRY: *And are you putting a lot of emphasis on how what they're doing relates to the world of work; how it'll come in useful there?*

WAYNE: *Probably not enough, no.*

HARRY: *Well there you are then, mate. That's two new things you can try. Off you go and get them engaged.*

Further reading

To read more about how to engage and motivate learners, see:

Wallace, S. (2007) *Getting the Buggers Motivated in FE*. London: Continuum.

E is for Engagement 2

How engaged do you feel with the work you do? How involved are you in decisions relating to your department, school or college, and what degree of control or influence do you have over your own working life?

These are questions that are increasingly being asked in all kind of organisations, including FE colleges. You may even have been asked them already as part of some internal staff survey or 'best employer' league table. But why does all this matter in the first place? After all, you turn up, do what you get paid for to the best of your ability. What more do they want?

Well, engagement is a big topic these days. It used to be called employee involvement, and before that it was probably wrapped up with what researchers called job satisfaction. So this is by no means a new concept, but it is one that seems regularly to feature as one of the 'hot topics' in organisations. The thinking goes something like this:

- » we all have a basic level of effort which is required to do our jobs satisfactorily (assuming we don't want to get sacked), but some of us give a lot more than this. The extra is what is called 'discretionary effort';

- » there are a number of reasons why we might do this, from blind ambition, or our own particular work ethic and personality, all the way to a desire to please our boss;

- » regardless of other factors, however, what we do know is that most of us work harder and more productively if:

  - our work appears meaningful to us (ie we feel part of something worthwhile and greater than ourselves);

  - we have some decision-making input into how our job is done;

  - we feel trusted, valued and recognised for our efforts.

The challenge of making work meaningful, of course, varies from organisation to organisation. According to research (CIPD, 2010), job satisfaction levels are highest in the health and social care sector and lowest in hotels and catering.

So, let's see how good a job your college does at generating engagement. Where would you place yourself (and maybe some of your colleagues) on Etzioni's scale of involvement (Etzioni, 1961)?

» **Moral Involvement** – *I believe wholeheartedly in the college's goals and values and feel hugely positive about my contribution to them.*

» **Calculative Involvement** – *So long as I can do a job I enjoy at a good salary with a decent pension at the end I'll happily give of my best.*

» **Compliant Involvement** – *I've been here long enough to feel part of the furniture, and whilst I frequently disagree with how they do things, I feel a certain sense of loyalty to the place, so I keep my nose clean.*

» **Alienative Involvement** – *The people who run this dump are a bunch of incompetent shysters, and even though I already do as little as possible, there are days I when I'd like to jack it all in. But then, frankly, who else would have me?*

There is ample research evidence to suggest that highly engaged staff not only work harder, but take the initiative and innovate more often, respond to change better, take less time off, provide better customer service, and are generally much better at coping with complex challenges. In 2009, the Secretary of State for Business commissioned a report by David MacLeod and Nita Clarke, called *Engaging for Success*, which looked at dozens of different organisations and arrived at the same conclusion. So it seems pretty obvious why increasing engagement is the holy grail of organisations and their senior managers. But what are the implications for the individual, other than voluntarily working a lot harder?

Well, I guess that rather depends on how cynical you are. The MacLeod report, among others, cites numerous examples of individual benefits, such as:

» improved well-being (greater control over work we find meaningful tends to reduce stress);

» increased job satisfaction (if we are satisfied by our work and therefore inclined to throw ourselves into it more, we are more likely to experience a sense of 'flow');

» feeling valued and trusted.

But whether you view this as a win-win objective or a cunning capitalist conspiracy, it is worth noting that the experts recognise that quick-fix, superficial approaches to staff engagement do not work. Organisations in which staff feel truly engaged have a complex and integrated set of factors built into their culture, processes and leadership style, which is robust and sustainable. However, in the interests of being helpful, and assuming you see some mileage in improving staff engagement in your department or college, here are some of the people management practices identified by the Chartered Institute of Personnel and Development (CIPD) as contributing to high engagement:

> » circulating information on performance and strategy;
> » providing all staff with a copy of the business plan and targets;
> » having an active staff association or union;
> » internal staff surveys;
> » staff suggestion schemes;
> » specific efforts on continuous improvement in work systems, such as quality circles/total quality management/Kaizen/Lean operation, self-managed or self-directed teams;
> » cross-function teams;
> » flexible working arrangements;
> » job rotation.

(CIPD, 2005)

At a more individual level, the Institute of Employment Studies (IES) has looked at what sort of management behaviours help or hinder staff engagement:

The Top Behaviours of Engaging Managers	The Top Behaviours of Disengaging Managers
Communicates, makes clear what is expected	Lacks empathy/interest in people
Listens, values and involves team	Fails to listen and communicate
Supportive, backs up team and individuals	Blames others, doesn't take responsibility
Target-focused	Doesn't motivate or inspire
Clear strategic vision	Self-centred
Shows active interest in others	Aggressive
Good leadership skills	Lacks awareness
Respected	Doesn't deliver

You may feel that you could have come up with that list without leaving your office, but it is always good to get common sense confirmed by research, and to see how so many of these good practices crop up in different contexts. Back to where we started this chapter, the challenge for you is two-fold.

1. How engaged do you feel in your work? How does this impact on you and others around you? What could you do to feel more engaged?

2. If you are in a position to influence the way your department or college is managed, what more could you be doing to raise levels of engagement amongst those that work with you?

E is for ETF

The Education and Training Foundation, originally known provisionally as the FE Guild, was registered as a corporation on 22 May 2013 and began operating in August of that year. It was created to take over the key functions of providing training and setting professional standards in FE, previously the responsibility of the now defunct Lifelong Learning UK (LLUK) and its standards arm, Standards and Verification UK (SVUK). In setting and policing professional standards for teachers and managers in the sector, the Foundation exerts a major influence on the working life of FE professionals at all levels. Part of its perceived role is to enhance the status of teachers and trainers in the sector. Its directors include representatives appointed by the Association of Colleges (AoC), the Association of Employment and Learning Providers (AELP) and the Association of Adult Education and Training Organisations (AAETO).

Further reading

For further information on the ETF see the Institute for Learning Website at www.ifl.ac.uk

F is for Feedback

A key skill not only in learner assessment but also in **M is for Mentoring, C is for Coaching, P is for Performance Management** and **I is for Interview** follow-up is giving feedback, an activity most of us approach with some trepidation. What often happens is that we criticise, our learner or appraisee gets defensive, so we justify ourselves, so they switch off, and the whole exercise ends in failure. Or we lavish undeserved praise on them because it's easier that way and nice to make somebody smile; but of course this gets us absolutely nowhere either in terms of our targets or the appraisee's development or performance.

The first thing we must recognise is that we are all hard-wired to be alert to danger and threat. The part of our brain which recognises and responds to this works faster than the part which analyses and processes information rationally. In fact, it's worse than this, because the part of our brain alert to threat, when aroused, actually inhibits the rational part. And what is one of the key threats we are sensitive to? Well, that would be threats to our status: that is to say, threats to our sense of how we are regarded by others. So it is small wonder that when someone says to us *I'd just like to give you a bit of feedback*, what we hear is *I'd just like to give you a bit of criticism*.

So good feedback technique is all about trying to take account of these natural responses and engage the individual's objective, rational thought processes. Here are some helpful hints:

When giving feedback:

» be PROMPT, whether it is positive or negative;

» create the right CONDITIONS. Feedback should take place in an atmosphere of trust and real rapport;

» ask QUESTIONS to enable them to assess themselves first;

» begin with two or three POSITIVE THINGS which you want to praise;

» follow with something that would make the performance even better next time;

» be SPECIFIC AND OBJECTIVE – give examples and reasons;

» don't be afraid to discuss how it makes you or them FEEL – good or bad;

» be clear about what the CONSEQUENCES of not improving their performance are;

» recognise what contribution you may have made to any problems;

» make clear your positive desire to HELP RESOLVE any problems;

» ask for THEIR RESPONSE to what you have said;

» finish with an OVERALL POSITIVE COMMENT. Consider getting them to summarise.

(Adapted from Wallace and Gravells, 2005)

Of course, the single biggest influence on the success of any feedback is probably the quality of the relationship you have with that person. If they trust and respect you, then you will have permission to offer quite critical feedback, because they believe you are 'on their side' and your intention is to help. If they do not believe this, then all the technique in the world will be of limited use.

F is for Foster Report

The report on the Foster Review of Further Education was published in November 2005. It is one example of the wide range of reports, reviews, consultations and **White Papers** whose recommendations, analyses or directives have a successive (and sometimes, it seems, all too frequent) impact on your working life as an FE manager. In the case of the Foster Report it is perhaps the *vision* put forward of FE – as a cornerstone of the Skills Sector – which should give us most pause for thought. After all, many working in FE – and this may include yourself – may not share exactly this vision of what it is they're about. It simply may not coincide with their own perception of their purpose, their identity or their role. For example, you may have colleagues whose motivation to teach in FE is driven by their belief in education for the sake of the individual rather than in skills training for the sake of the economy. There is always a danger with *visions* that they may not be unanimously shared. Not everyone may buy into them; and this is particularly a risk when the vision appears to be imposed from above or – as in this case – from outside the college altogether. One of the requirements of a professional is the ability to navigate through the squalls caused by philosophical and political positionings such as these, steering in the required direction while maintaining a 'happy ship' in which everyone's right to a point of view is valued. This needs more than **E is for Emotional Intelligence**; it requires you to see things coming. And that in turn means keeping updated by familiarising yourself with the contents of the reviews, reports and **W is for White Papers** pertaining to the FE sector as and when they appear (see **U is for Updating**).

It's interesting to note that Foster describes FE not as a **C is for Cinderella**, but as a *Middle Child*. This alternative metaphor may be a useful one to you. It is presumably intended to position the sector between schools (youngest child) and HE (oldest) while pointing out that it is often, undeservedly, neglected in favour of the other two. Well, at least it gets us out of the realms of pantomime.

G is for Grading

There are two senses in which grading can be an issue of concern when you're working in FE. The one that probably causes most anxiety is Ofsted's grading of individual performance (see also **I is for Inspection** and **O is for Observations**). This may seem a bit of a lottery, dependent on the day, the class and your general levels of anxiety. It is judgemental rather than developmental (that is, it grades you as a teacher, based on that particular session). It is not designed as diagnostic feedback to support you in your professional development. Being graded as a professional based on a brief snapshot of your professional practice is likely to cause you some degree of stress. Under such circumstances you may find it helpful to read **S is for Stress** and **R is for Resilience.** You can keep up-to-date with Ofsted grading terminology and descriptors by checking the Ofsted Website: www.ofsted.gov.uk.

The other sense in which you may be concerned with grading is in the assessment of learners' work. In general, however, the vocational curriculum tends to operate on a *competent or not competent* model which doesn't involve giving a grade. Some argue that there are some disadvantages to this. For example, the fact that there's no distinction made between 'very competent' and 'barely competent' may discourage learners from doing their very best, and provides no indication to prospective employers of an applicant's capacity for excellence. This argument is based on the assumption that grades are useful both as a reward and as an objective indicator of excellence.

For courses which do involve grading, detailed grading criteria and descriptors will be provided by the awarding body or institution, and moderation processes will be in place across and within centres of delivery to ensure that the assessment decisions and grading outcomes are rigorous and standardised. If you have not had previous experience of grading learners' work, these systems will be there to support you.

H is for HE in FE

Increasingly, higher education courses and qualifications are being offered in FE colleges, often in collaboration with a local university. Foundation degrees are now part of the provision at many colleges; usually a two-year course and focusing on vocationally related areas of study. Foundation degrees were first introduced in 2001 and are awarded across a range of subjects, such as sciences (FdSc), law (FdL), education (FdEd) and engineering (FdE). Successful graduates of the foundation degree can 'top up' their qualification, usually at a university, to convert it to an honours degree. The purpose behind setting up this provision was to create a more highly skilled workforce, which is one reason why its natural home is the FE sector. It mainly recruits 20- to 30-year-olds who have not followed the usual academic route into HE.

Teaching HE in FE demands skills and teaching styles which might be quite different from those you would use to support, for example, 17-year-olds on level 2 courses (see **C is for Critical Thinking**). Not only will the students be older (see **Adult learners**), but also the curriculum content will be more complex and demanding. This will have a direct impact on the teacher's role, requiring them to adapt and extend their existing skills set, as Head of Faculty, Jason, explains to Harry:

JASON: *You'll be fine. You're just the person we need to be teaching on this degree. It's one of our flagship courses. I saw the students for a session last week and they're a great group. Only 12 of them, but all dead keen.*

HARRY: *I keep worrying what's going to happen if they know more than I do!*

JASON: *You know as well as I do that you've got the subject knowledge. Obviously it'll be as important as ever to keep yourself up-to-date, and probably to a greater depth. But what might seem unfamiliar at first isn't what you're going to be teaching, but how you teach it. You can expect these students to be much more responsive in group discussions for example. And they'll be hungry for information, so there'll be more scope for exposition and lectures. We know that with youngsters it's sometimes difficult to get them to discuss anything; with this lot it's a case of having to stop them and move them on. I think you'll enjoy extending your professional skills, and I think they'll enjoy your teaching. You're one of the best.*

HARRY: *It's the assessment that worries me.*

JASON: *There are very clear assessment criteria and descriptors, and the university joins with us for cross-moderation. But yes, it's a different ball game in some ways, particularly the level and scope of formative feedback that you'll need to provide, and also the way you provide it. Some of these students have been out of education and training for quite a while. They may be on our highest level course, but they'll still need a lot of support and reassurance about getting back into formal learning again.*

Jason's advice is sound. But it's also important to remember that good teaching, the ability to effectively support learners, is a transferable skill. Your lesson planning will always take account of the characteristics and needs of the learners you are designing it for. The fact that your learners are on an advanced or degree level course doesn't alter the principles of good professional practice, which are:

» conscientious preparation, including keeping your subject knowledge updated;

» careful planning designed to meet learners' needs and preferred learning styles;

» enthusiastic and engaging delivery;

» interesting and relevant learner activities;

» prompt and constructive assessment.

(See also **F is for Feedback**.)

H is for Human Resources

Human resources are people. You yourself are a human resource and, hopefully, by browsing this A–Z, you are in the process of making yourself an even more valuable and effective one. It is often argued that in FE every manager is a human resource (HR) manager because every manager is, in one way or another, managing people. Whatever your specific role at the moment, you will need to know something about:

» the role of the HR manager in FE;

» the HR responsibilities of an FE line manager (someone in a post like yours, perhaps).

In the days before incorporation in 1993, few FE college organisational structures included posts for human resource or personnel managers because Local Authorities (at that time known as Local Education Authorities: LEAs) were responsible for the human resourcing and personnel functions. However, since colleges have grown into their role as corporate bodies and have taken responsibility for the recruitment and management of their staff, the HR function has become a central and key part of college management structures.

The functions of the HR manager include:

» staff recruitment, selection and contractual arrangements;

» maintaining a balance between organisational and individual performance. This will include such things as annual reviews and appraisals, staff training and development;

» staff relations and industrial relations (for example, issues involving trade unions), health and safety issues, and **D is for Disciplinary** procedures.

One of the requirements of an HR manager in FE is a working knowledge of employment law and the college policies that interpret it. Since incorporation, colleges have needed to develop a wide range of HR policies in order to undertake their HR responsibilities under the terms of their articles of incorporation, and in order to comply with employment law nationally. Typically these policies will cover such areas as **R is for Recruitment**, redundancy, discipline and equal opportunities. These policies and HR specialists, however, do not take away the responsibility of all line managers in FE (and this may include you) to manage their own teams effectively, fairly and in line with current legislation. It is the line manager's responsibility to follow exactly the procedures set down in college policy and to ensure that the colleagues they manage have access to all necessary guidelines and that they receive appropriate advice as necessary.

I is for Inclusion

You have, of course, like any good professional, familiarised yourself with your college's policy on inclusion. As with the anti-bullying policy, you'll need a working knowledge of the current regulations and required procedures in case you are called upon to respond to incidents or allegations which fall under the categories covered by the policy. There are also background issues about inclusion in FE, however, of which you need to remain mindful.

The traditional profile of managers, particularly senior managers, in the FE sector has been predominantly white and male. While the same is true of other organisations and institutions, the pattern persisted in FE longer than might have been hoped. This has resulted in it being a recurring issue on the agenda of national bodies such as Ofsted and led to initiatives such as the Learning and Skill Council (2001–10) undertaking to the Commission for Black Staff in FE to encourage and support FE colleges in modelling best race equality practice as employers.

On an individual scale, inclusion presents a number of challenges. These may be personal and professional ones about career trajectory and progression, and there may well be issues to address about role modelling. If you work in a college where managers are predominantly white or predominantly male, or, for example, include none with a disability, or where that pattern is evident in the most senior positions, you will need to consider the possible effects on the career aspirations of learners or of those members of your team who may see themselves as marginalised in relation to the dominant groups. The same principle applies where management or senior management teams are seen as predominantly or exclusively able-bodied, heterosexual, under 40 or over 50. The thing to remember is that, despite the best intentions of a college's inclusion policy, inequality of opportunity can nevertheless appear implicit in an organisation where members of particular groups are never or rarely seen in leadership or management positions. It can lead to learner disengagement and to talented professionals leaving the college on the assumption that they'll get nowhere if they stay.

At a programme leader and team leader level, it can also have a critical impact on student recruitment, retention and achievement, for example in curriculum areas which were traditionally thought of as gender-specific (such as Nursery Nursing or Trowel Trades). An all-male teaching team and hierarchy in the engineering section could be a factor in discouraging the recruitment of women learners, or contributing to low retention rates (or low achievement rates) among women learners. And the converse is equally possible in a health and social care school with an exclusively female staffing profile. With the current emphasis on targets, such issues need some consideration.

The extent to which you can address any of this directly will depend on your position and seniority within the college. As a teacher or first-line manager leading a small team, you can ensure that those whom you work with and those whom you teach feel valued as individuals and – if necessary – are exposed to a diverse and balanced range of role models, for example through mentoring arrangements, visits, continuing professional development programmes and contacts with outside bodies.

Another term for inclusion is *social justice*. It is about enabling all learners to participate fully in education and training, and about reducing inequalities that exist for the socially disadvantaged. It is central, too, to provision for learners with special educational or training needs. The Salamanca Statement of 1994 identified this provision as a social justice issue, calling for the use of the term 'inclusion' in this context, to replace the old term, 'integration', which implied the need to fit learners into provision which represented a 'norm'.

I is for Influencing

You may be a junior member of the department, not long out of teacher training, full of bright ideas and wanting to make a difference to your college. You may be a more experienced senior lecturer, given the opportunity to lead a cross-curricular project with colleagues over whom you have no formal authority. Or you may be a head of department, promoted over equally experienced colleagues, who is trying to find a style of leadership which motivates and preserves the respect of your team.

In all of these situations, you may be required to call upon your powers of influence and persuasion.

You may feel wary of such terms, conjuring up as they do the unscrupulous time-share salesman or mealy-mouthed politician. Moreover, we are more easily influenced by people that have power over us. But none of these create the conditions for sustainable influence. So let us be clear what we mean.

Influencing is the process of making our ideas and opinions attractive to others by dint of understanding their needs and wants, earning their trust and respect, and communicating appropriately and effectively.

This is not about manipulation, propaganda or coercion.

Consequently, all the skills and practices of good communication form the bedrock for influencing (see **C is for Challenging**, **I is for Interviews**, **L is for Listening** and **N is for Negotiation**). But to these we can add some helpful insights into developing productive relationships and managing the process of influencing. Empathy, the ability to put ourselves in another's shoes and understand what they need and want, is central to this. So, perhaps unsurprisingly the first question to ask ourselves is this:

What is it that we find persuasive when someone is trying to influence us?

Well, the truth is we are more easily persuaded by people we like and respect, so being a positive, helpful, competent and reliable colleague, team member or manager will give you a head start. How do you think *you* are regarded by those whom you seek to influence?

Furthermore, we are more likely to be persuaded by someone who takes the trouble to understand what *we* want and need. This is because we are also more easily persuaded by those willing to *do a deal*. How would you view someone who actively sought out ways of creating reciprocal benefits versus someone who just presented their case and then stuck to it through thick and thin? And yet so often when setting out to persuade, we marshall all our arguments and then bombard the other party with an overwhelming barrage of points in favour. What is it like to be on the receiving end of this? Persuasive? No, I thought not.

Influence, therefore, is as much about asking good QUESTIONS (and listening to the answers) as it is about making powerful statements (see **I is for Interviews** for ideas on good questioning). Try to establish what outcomes and benefits are most important to those you seek to influence. Where is the most mutually beneficial result to be found?

How else can we structure our communication to maximise its power of influence? Here are a few thoughts:

> » organise your thoughts and express them clearly;
>
> » try to use examples wherever possible;
>
> » offer real benefits;
>
> » stress the positive aspects, but don't try to hide the negatives;
>
> » where your idea has been successfully applied elsewhere, explain this.

Sarah, the head of faculty for sports and leisure, is trying to get Norman, one of her heads of school, to adopt a more assertive approach to performance management with his team:

NORMAN: *I can't understand it really. I called Raj in to my office on Monday, and I said to him 'Raj', I said, I said 'Raj, could it not possibly be that you're nothing like as good as you seem to think you are? I mean, I'm sorry, but, you know, you might get good feedback on your classroom performance, but, well, admin-wise, maybe it would help if you got these exam scores in on time like I asked. Perhaps you could give a bit more thought to the boring clerical stuff like the rest of us ...' Well, he just looked at me like he does, you know ...*

SARAH: *Why do you think he acts like this Norman? He's a pretty good section leader. What's in it for him being so casual about his paperwork?*

NORMAN: *Absolutely no idea. I don't suppose I'll ever know what's going on inside his head, probably. I mean how could I?*

SARAH: *What do you think would happen if you asked him?*

NORMAN: *Umm ... well, sorry, but I'm not sure I follow ...*

SARAH: *Look, you're a sociable chap Norman, and it's important to you that you're liked by your team. I know that. But could it be you're confusing being sensitive with just beating around the bush? Raj is not like you. He's very ambitious, impatient and easily bored. He's clearly got the impression that admin is somehow an unimportant element and will not affect assessment of his performance. If you want to guarantee building a lasting productive relationship with him, then flatter his ego, praise him for what he does well, stop mincing your words and make him commit to action where he needs to improve.*

NORMAN: *Well, that's all very well for you to say, but Raj can be quite bolshie when he wants to be ...*

SARAH: *Look Norman, I know this stuff makes you anxious, but let's just try one thing, and I guarantee your relationship with Raj will be much less troublesome. Sit him down and say to him 'Raj, you're a bloody good lecturer and looked up to as such by everyone in the department, but it is a fact that I will assess your management performance as unsatisfactory unless you give admin deadlines the priority and attention they deserve. You will be as respected for your management abilities as you are for your teaching, if only you get things like exam scores in on time, starting immediately. Can I have your commitment to this here and now?'*

What is different about Norman's approach to influencing and Sarah's? Look back over the conversation above and jot a few notes down.

First, Norman has not taken the trouble to understand Raj and his personality and motivation. Sarah, on the other hand, not only understands Norman pretty well, but seems to know his team member better than he does too. She appreciates the need to ask questions. Consequently, she knows that Norman needs to take things slowly and one step at a time. He needs lots of reassurance, reinforcement and structure. Raj too needs his ego stroking. Prestige and status are important to him. He is proactive and assertive himself and will appreciate this in others. He hates beating around the bush, and likes to make quick decisions. Look at the way Sarah influences Norman, and the way she suggests he deal with Raj.

Finally, look at the language Sarah and Norman use. What do you notice? Whilst Norman's talk is peppered with 'weak' words and conditional phrases (maybe, possibly, sorry, perhaps, suppose, etc.) Sarah's mode of address is far more definite and powerful (I know, clearly, will, guarantee, stop, commit, fact, etc.).

So, let's summarise what makes for effective influencing:

> » gain rapport and trust;

> » ask questions and listen carefully;

> » try to understand what the other person wants and needs;

- » take account of different styles and personalities;
- » identify reciprocal benefits and stress these;
- » mind your language – use 'powerful' not 'weak' words and phrases;
- » move assertively towards a decision.

I is for Inspection

There is an Ofsted inspection coming up at Bogginbrook College, and while Sheena is using her one free hour of the week to sort out some pre-inspection documentation in the office, she overhears the following conversation between the VP and Parveen, her head of school, as they stand talking in the foyer.

PARVEEN: *The trouble is, I'm having to do everything myself.*

VP: *Surely you can get the people in your school to sort out some of the paperwork?*

PARVEEN: *Well yes, you'd think so. Wouldn't you? But the trouble is I just wouldn't be able to trust them to get it done. They're hopeless. I wouldn't be surprised if they set out to sabotage the whole thing.*

VP: *Why on earth would they do that?*

PARVEEN: *To get at me. After all, the inspection grade is going to reflect on me and how I run this school. It's not going to bother them, is it?*

VP: *Well ...*

PARVEEN: *And I just hope Sheena doesn't set out to rock the boat. I wouldn't put it past her.*

VP: *Oh dear. I didn't realise.*

We all know that Parveen is wrong here on a number of counts. Inspections *aren't* there as an opportunity for managers to set out on an ego trip or to try to show that they run their section, school or department single-handed. Indeed, part of the purpose of inspections is to evaluate team effectiveness. And they *do* have an impact on the stress levels and self-esteem of individual teachers and teaching teams. And we know that Sheena is conscientiously pulling her weight. What's happening here is that Parveen is openly demonstrating a) that she is stressed beyond the point where she can act rationally or with discretion; and b) that she has – unjustly – no faith in her team to rise to the occasion or behave professionally. These are the two worst mistakes a manager can make when preparing for an inspection.

Before incorporation, FE colleges were subject to occasional inspections by HMI (Her Majesty's Inspectorate) and by their LEA (Local Education Authority) inspectors. After incorporation, inspection has become almost a way of life, with inspections at first carried out by the FEFC (FE Funding Council) inspectorate, and then subsequently by Ofsted and the Adult Learning Inspectorate (2001–07) (later subsumed into Ofsted). One of the most productive – but also from an FE professional's point of view most time-consuming – practices to have arisen from the current inspection regime is the college self-assessment. The regular cycle of self assessments will inevitably involve you, whatever your role, in a number of additional activities including audits and observations. Here are three pieces of advice that will be helpful to you in preparing for a self-assessment exercise or a formal Ofsted inspection.

» Ofsted inspection reports on FE colleges are posted on *the Ofsted Website* and make very useful reading. Certain themes emerge there. For example, inspections in several colleges may discover difficulties in the effective management of small teams, or poor communication within or between designated teams. From your point of view this is valuable intelligence. It alerts you to which areas of practice may come under particular scrutiny, and allows you to examine and revise policies and practices within your own team.

» Everyone is certain to feel increased levels of stress when facing an inspection. Even if this is 'only' a self-assessment, it's likely to involve graded observations of their teaching. While you yourself may feel snowed under with paperwork, meetings and other administrative duties generated by assessments and inspections, you will still need to remember that every individual in your team is having their own reaction to process, and it's highly unlikely that anyone is entirely immune to the general sense of stress which inspections generate. So, however stretched you feel, if you have any leadership responsibility for your subject or for a whole team, this still calls for a sympathetic attitude on your part and a great deal of cheerleading, morale-boosting and confidence-building. All three of these are more easily accomplished when there are good working relationships. The worst possible line to take is the one Parveen takes with Sheena.

» Keep in mind that there is a clear distinction between observations of teaching carried out for developmental purposes, as in annual reviews and appraisals or on CPD programmes, for example, and those carried out for judgemental purposes, as in a self-assessment or inspection. Although both have the declared purpose of contributing towards an improvement in practice, from the point of view of the teacher being observed, judgmental feedback (*This is your grade. This categorises your current level of skill as a teacher*) feels very different from developmental feedback (*This is what I saw. Do you feel there are ways you'd like to improve on this?*). Whether the observations are performed by yourself or by an inspector, it is always important to *ensure that judgements made are discussed and acted on in such a way as to raise quality of provision rather than lower teacher morale* (see **F is for Feedback** and **O is for Observations**).

For the latest Ofsted reports on FE colleges go to: www.ofsted.gov.uk.

I is for Interviews

Among the most crucial skills for anyone whose job depends on working with other people is that of having productive one-to-one conversations. These may be members of your team, colleagues, prospective employees, outside agencies or students. The context may be recruitment, coaching, appraisal, discipline, negotiation or joint problem-solving. But there are certain core skills which you can learn once and apply in all of these situations. These are:

» managing the environment;

» building rapport;

» recognising non-verbal cues;

» asking good questions;

» active listening;

» closing.

Managing the environment

This is all about creating the appropriate conditions for a successful conversation. Generally this means the following:

» conduct your interviews in a place which is comfortable but business-like (ie not on hard chairs in a bare, windowless office, but equally not sitting on the bed in a hotel room);

» find a place where you will not be overheard or interrupted. Respect people's need for confidentiality. Telephones should be diverted, and ideally the door closed or even a 'Please do not disturb' sign clearly displayed on the door. Mobile phones and pagers should be switched off;

» try to arrange the furniture in such a way as to make you both feel at ease and free to talk. Interviews conducted across desks are to be avoided, as are different types or levels of seating;

» be on time. It is discourteous to people to do otherwise.

Building rapport

Productive conversations usually depend upon an open and honest exchange of information, and you are more likely to get this if you devote some effort to helping the other person relax. Even negotiation and disciplinary encounters are best addressed as opportunities for mutual problem-solving, and this usually means finding common ground.

> » Avoid leaping straight in with tough questions or challenges. Give the other person an opportunity to relax and settle into the interview. Indulge in small talk. Find something they are comfortable talking about.

> » It is useful to begin with an explanation of the nature and structure of the interview, what you want to discuss, and an idea of how long it is intended to last.

> » Try to match your body language with theirs, but maintain an open posture, avoiding defensive gestures such as crossed arms.

> » Maintain regular eye contact.

> » If taking notes during the interview, inform the interviewee in advance.

> » Invite questions.

Recognising non-verbal cues

There are those who have made a detailed study of this topic, and claim to read all sorts of covert messages into our every look and gesture. But for us lay people, the important thing to remember is that less than 10 per cent of communication may be conveyed by the actual words we say (Mehrabian, 1972). The other thing to remember is that common sense can go a long way.

> » Conversation means taking turns. Learning to recognise what people do when they feel it's their turn can help us manage how much we say. This includes leaning forward, clearing their throat, raising their head and opening their lips, among other things. We all know people who are resolutely blind to all these cues, and you do not want to get next to them at a party.

> » Watch out for changes of facial expression. Frowning, for example, may indicate lack of understanding or disagreement. It may be time for a question. Taut facial muscles and pursed lips may indicate you are on the wrong tack.

> » Similarly we may able to detect how engaged someone is with what we are saying by whether they lean forward and look animated or dissociate themselves by leaning back and looking away.

Asking good questions

Let us remind ourselves of some of the different sorts of questions and how we might use them.

Open questions – questions that require more than a simple yes or no answer.

> » Tell me about ...

> » What would you like to discuss?

> » How did you feel about ...?

These are the questions that are great for exploring issues and getting information, so good interviewers tend to use them most.

Probe questions – questions that follow up a topic in more detail.

> » What do you mean when you say ...?

> » Tell me a bit more about ...?

> » How do you know ...?

Good for finding out more detail or challenging glib statements, these are used to ensure that issues have been fully examined, and assumptions not taken for granted.

Hypothetical questions – these questions open the mind to new possibilities.

> » What if you were to ...?

> » What would be the consequences if ...?

> » How would you feel about ...?

Useful for testing people's position on an issue, or their commitment to a course of action, but beware, these questions can allow job applicants to impress with what they *might* have done, instead of what they *did* do. They can also turn into leading questions (see below).

Link questions – questions which seek to understand the connection between ideas and events.

> » So, if you say you cannot do ... what will that mean for ...?

> » How will you ... if ...?

> » You say you do this, and that this often happens ... Are these two things connected?

These are good for prompting new understanding and helping someone explore cause and effect.

Closed questions – questions that generally have a yes or no answer. Excessive use of these can turn a conversation into a session of 20 questions, particularly with someone who is shy or inclined to be monosyllabic. Used in moderation, however, for clarification or probing, they can help to avoid misunderstandings.

> » So this happened last week?
>
> » Are you saying you have tried this?
>
> » Will you have this done by ...?

Leading questions – questions which invite a particular answer by the way they are phrased.

> » So, do you think your problem is ...?
>
> » I expect you were just feeling a bit off, were you?
>
> » I guess at that point you ... did you?

These are to be avoided, generally, as they disguise the facts and smack of manipulation.

Active listening

In any one-to-one interchange, it is not enough just to listen. We have to show we are listening. This is often referred to as 'active listening'.

Active listening is the skill of concentrating on what someone is saying and demonstrating that you have heard and understood what they have said. Here is a reminder of some of the ways we can listen actively.

> » Do not start thinking of your next question as soon as you've asked the previous one.
>
> » If you must write notes, try to keep them brief, or stop the conversation to write them.
>
> » Do not be afraid of silence.
>
> » Do not interrupt, but if things are getting off the point, steer the discussion back at the first available opportunity, perhaps by saying, *I'm sorry may I ask about something else?*

» Watch your body language. Remember, leaning forward and nodding demonstrates interest. Leaning back, folding your arms and looking at the ceiling does not.

» Make encouraging noises (uh-huh … right … yes … I see … tell me more … really?).

» Summarise to help check understanding.

» In most cases you should aim for the other person to talk for at least 70 per cent of the time.

Closing

Any productive conversation should have an outcome. Do not finish one without articulating what this is.

» Summarise what has been discussed. Check for mutual understanding.

» Ensure you both leave with an agreed outcome, ideally some action, even if this is that you need to meet again.

» Say what will happen next, along with any communication processes and what timescales can be expected.

J is for JFDI

An acronym that will already be familiar to many, JFDI stands for *Just Flipping Do It*, or words to that effect. Its relevance here is three-fold.

First, as a general rule, we all learn to recognise when the discussion and mulling over and planning must give way to the process of actually doing something. Sheena has suggested to Parveen that some changes to the delivery of the Care Management NVQ programme may enable more convenient timetabling. As a result, she's got the job of doing it.

» She has agreed clear objectives as to what will be delivered (see **O is for Objectives**).

» Perhaps she has assembled a competent project team composed of relevant people.

» She may have identified local 'champions' around the college who will help.

» She has agreed who is accountable for what and clarified the limits of her own authority.

» She has (hopefully) devised success criteria that will ultimately tell her whether she has achieved what she planned to.

» She has maybe analysed who the stakeholders are in this issue, and who will support, who will put up resistance and who will be neutral.

» She has clearly communicated what she wants to do, and tried to manage people's expectations.

» She has set out a process for monitoring progress towards the objectives.

In other words, she has dutifully followed many of the rules of good project management.

But she will not have all the information she would like and, because life is occasionally unpredictable, she will never have accounted for everything. We must therefore recognise the point at which the only way to learn more is to take action and see what happens. As soon as we start to implement anything we change things (see **C is for Change**), and because things in organisations are interconnected, this may change the entire 'playing field' on which we are operating, affect people's responses and support (or lack of it) and therefore affect the way we wish to proceed with our project. Retaining this flexibility means knowing when to stop initial planning, try something, see what happens, and learn from it for the rest of the plan. This is why many successful projects start with a pilot or trial, because often the only way to see what works is to try it. *A bad decision is better than no decision* has become a management cliché, but it captures a significant truth. The idea that lots of small, related change activities can reach a point where much wider systemic change in an organisation is accelerated stems from recent concepts such as chaos theory and 'tipping points'. These have been applied to various phenomena, including climate change.

Second, these thoughts may also be relevant to those faced with yet another 'strategic initiative', launched from on high, outside the college itself.

It is always tempting in such circumstances to do your King Lear impression, railing against the elements to whichever poor colleague happens to have wandered by. If you feel that there is about as much chance of government listening to you as there was the storm listening to Lear, then here's an alternative strategy. Express your professional opinion, by all means, then move through the kind of planning disciplines mentioned above (sometimes this very process can expose fatal flaws in the project), but then, importantly, take some action and get a result. At least you will feel in control, and if no one else chooses to learn from the outcomes, at least you will.

Which brings us to our third application of JFDI: your own self-development. We all know people's learning styles vary, and some have a greater preference for experimentation than others. But, whatever learning style we find most comfortable, the learning cycle (Kolb, 1983) cannot function without us taking action. A desire to make the perfect plan, or an understandable fear of failure can hold us back, but we know from experience with our students that having a go, learning from it and trying a different tack is more conducive to development and personal growth. The same goes for managers, which is why our reaction to our team's mistakes can have such an impact on the culture we create.

K is for Kinaesthetic Learners

Kinaesthetic learners are those who prefer to learn through activity. Many learners in FE demonstrate this preference. They learn best when they are able to move about, rather than remain seated for entire lessons. They benefit from observing a demonstration of what they're required to do before trying to perform the task themselves. This method of demonstration and practice is a useful one to incorporate into lesson plans for groups in which kinaesthetic learners predominate. If you have learners in your class who seem to have more energy than they know what to do with, make sure you build plenty of practical activities into your planning – preferably ones which needn't require the learners to sit still in one place. We sometimes refer to this preferred style of learning as 'learning by doing'. It is therefore well-suited to a competence-based vocational curriculum such as we have in FE.

(See also **S is for Styles of Learning**.)

L is for Leadership

What do we mean when we talk about leadership, and is a leader different from a manager? To what extent are we all leaders in our own way?

Many commentators, among them Warren Bennis and John Kotter, both American academics, have drawn a clear distinction between management and leadership. These comparisons generally portray management as a somewhat static, rule-bound and transactional process for ensuring that things get done efficiently. Leadership, on the other hand, is an altogether more sexy approach, which involves creating a compelling vision of the future, inspiring followers, developing people and promoting continuous change.

In his book, *On Becoming a Leader* (1989), Bennis associates management with administration, systems, structure, control and maintaining the status quo. In contrast, leadership he sees as being about innovation, development, people, inspiring trust, taking the long view and challenging the accepted way of doing things. However, ultimately, we see these sorts of distinctions as potentially unhelpful to staff in colleges, at all levels, trying to do their best to meet conflicting demands from a variety of stakeholders. Making a kind of 'second-class citizen' out of the necessary work of sound execution and delivery undervalues the work of diligent managers toiling away at making things happen, sometimes against the odds. Rather than making management and leadership appear mutually exclusive, it might be more helpful to see these definitions, as Kotter does, as complementary parts of a single role, at whatever level it is practised. After all, there are surely not many organisations that have jobs for 'managers' who cannot inspire, motivate and develop their teams, or for 'leaders' who can communicate a compelling vision of the future, but cannot ensure the steps are put in place to get there.

In other words, transactional and transformational leadership are two parts of the same model (Bass, 1998; Avolio, 1999). In simple terms, transactional leadership is an exchange, as the name suggests. As manager, you understand what your team members want, and you agree roles and responsibilities, behaviours and performance standards, in return for which they are rewarded, through praise, pay, promotion, etc. You can achieve this by simply monitoring performance, and telling people off when they get it wrong ('management by exception'), or, better yet, you can put the focus on recognising and rewarding people when they *do* achieve what is expected of them ('contingent reward').

So, *what's wrong with transactional leadership?* you may be asking yourself. The answer is nothing. This model is not about either-or. Having clear roles and responsibilities, SMART objectives and standards of performance, and taking the trouble to praise positive behaviour and address under-performance is all good stuff. It generally beats having no structure or standards and just letting everyone do what they like ('laissez-faire leadership'). However, the proposition is that management effectiveness is hugely increased when transactional leadership is supplemented by transformational leadership. (In its 2005 report, *Leadership, Development and Diversity in the Learning and Skills Sector*, the Learning and Skills Research Centre concluded that successful organisations differed in their approach to leadership. Although a transformational leadership style was considered most effective in improving performance and in leading for diversity, managers in the sector were seen as more often employing a transactional approach.)

Transformational leaders command the trust, respect and admiration to be positive role models for their teams. They have a sense of purpose, which they share with their team, and they display determination and conviction in pursuing this. Part of this 'idealised influence' may be what people refer to as charisma, but it may also be the result of more tangible behaviours.

Transformational leaders are optimistic and positive. They paint an attractive picture of the future, and make people's work meaningful and challenging. They have high expectations.

Transformational leaders help people look at old problems in new ways, by asking challenging questions and making us think more creatively.

Finally, transformational leaders remember to focus on individual learning and development needs as well, by mentoring and coaching, delegating, and just walking around talking to people (see **C is for Coaching**, **D is for Delegation**, **M is for Mentoring** and **W is for Walking Around**).

Usually, when we are asked to think of great leaders (and actually when we are asked to think of great teachers), we think of these transformational qualities. It is argued that leaders who display these behaviours enable followers to achieve beyond their expectations, whereas a transactional approach will, at best, only achieve the expected outcome. Provided a degree of structure and support is in place, transformational leaders are more likely to allow people the freedom to think for themselves. (Laissez-faire leaders will just leave them to flounder, then blame them when they get it wrong.)

Transformational leadership is not an alternative to transactional leadership. Rather it is a way of adding to its effectiveness. We must develop both transactional and transformational skills, because in truth, successful institutions need people at all levels who can both inspire and deliver.

The idea that leadership behaviour can be found and developed at all levels is sometimes referred to as 'distributed leadership', and used in conjunction with this idea of transactional and transformational leadership, it begins to build a way of looking at leadership which has relevance for us whatever our job title.

L is for Learning Outcomes

Trainee teacher Madge bumps into her mentor, Zoe.

ZOE: *Madge! Hi! Thanks for writing up your bit of the scheme of work. Could I just have a quick chat to you about how we set out learning objectives?*

MADGE: *Oh no! I've done something wrong, haven't I?*

ZOE: *Don't get into a flap. I just want to explain something. Sit down. Now, look. When we write learning outcomes we have to make sure that they are observable – that they're expressed in terms of what the learners should be able to do by the end of the lesson. OK?*

MADGE: *OK.*

ZOE: *Now, why do you think we have to word them in that way?*

MADGE: *Erm. Because then we know what we have to assess to see whether the learner's achieved the outcome?*

ZOE: *Absolutely! Good. So now can you tell me what the problem is with this outcome as you've written it on your lesson plan: 'To understand the booking procedure.' What's the problem with that, from the point of view of assessment?*

MADGE: *Erm. No. I don't know.*

ZOE: *OK. How will you be able to assess whether the learner understands the procedure?*

MADGE: *Uh! I see! I won't, will I? I can't really assess whether they understand something unless I get them to explain it to me. So what I should have written was: 'To* explain *the booking procedure.'*

ZOE: *Yes. But better still: 'To explain the booking procedure* correctly.*' And it helps if you remember that all lesson learning outcomes should have the prefix: 'By the end of the lesson the learner will be able to....'*

Learning outcomes, learning objectives, competence statements: they should all be written in terms of what the learner should be able to do by the end of that learning process. The outcomes drive the lesson plan. They dictate the types of learner activity required in order to achieve those outcomes *and demonstrate them* so that they can be assessed. As Zoe points out, words such as 'understand' or 'know' or 'learn' aren't useful for this purpose. They don't describe observable, assessable activities, and so they create a lack of clarity about how and at what points in the lesson the outcomes will be assessed. Descriptors such as 'correctly' or 'accurately' are also important for standards of assessment.

Further reading

For more discussion of learning outcomes and how they fit into lesson planning you could look at:

Wallace, S. (2011) *Teaching, Tutoring and Training in the LLS* (4th Edition). Exeter: Learning Matters.

L is for Lesson Planning

Trainee teacher Madge feels in need of some advice from her mentor, Zoe.

MADGE: *Help!*

ZOE: *Hello, there, Madge. You look very red in the face and worried. Again. What's up?*

MADGE: *I'm working on my lesson plan for my session tomorrow when my tutor's coming in to observe me and assess my practical teaching. But it's just I've been talking to Norman and he says there's no point doing lesson plans and he never does them and when I'm a real teacher I won't bother.*

ZOE: *I think Norman's just teasing you. I wouldn't take that too seriously. Careful planning's absolutely essential to good teaching; and people who say they just have a plan in their head are missing the point. Lesson planning's a developmental process. It makes you think about what you're doing. Are you doing too much talking? Are the learners getting enough changes of activity? Have you allowed for differentiation? All that sort of thing. And if the lesson went well, you've got a map of it to look back on so that you can reflect on why it succeeded. And then you know what works well for next time.*

MADGE: *And if it goes badly ...*

ZOE: *I'm sure it won't. But yes, if it goes badly, you've got that plan of it there so that you can identify where it went wrong and what you might try differently another time. People with some sketchy notes on the back of an old envelope don't have that advantage. Do you want me to have a look at what you've planned so far?*

Zoe is right. Lesson planning, if it's done well, is one of a teacher's best assets. Not only does it provide a set of cues or memory aids to remind us of what to do next, but it also provides a point of comparison for later reflection. The process of planning allows us to consider questions such as:

» Have I included enough activities to keep the learners active and engaged?

» What specific learner activities do I need to include in order to be able to assess whether lesson outcomes have been met?

» What assessment opportunities have I built in?

» Is it sufficiently inclusive? Do the learner activities allow for differentiation of task and/or outcome?

» Do my timings look realistic?

» Am I, as teacher, going to be doing too much talking?

After the lesson, the plan allows the teacher to reflect on questions such as the following:

» Did the lesson turn out that way or did circumstances force a change of plan? And if so, why and how?

» Which particular parts of the lesson were the most successful? Might this work equally well with a different group of learners?

» Did anything in the plan not work out? If so, why, and what could I do differently another time?

» Was the lesson plan appropriate to the characteristics of this group of learners? How does it take these characteristics into account?

You will always encounter people like Norman who tell you plans aren't necessary or are only for trainee teachers. Try asking them how they got by without a plan at the last Ofsted inspection or college self-assessment exercise. You can bet they did a bit of planning then.

(See also **L is for Learning Outcomes**.)

L is for Listening

When was the last time you really listened to someone? I mean *really* listened?

Here's another question then: when is the last time someone really listened to *you*?

Listening is a bit like driving a car. Without thinking, we regard ourselves as much better at it than everyone else. So we assume that we are a pretty good listener, whilst complaining that no one ever listens to us. Of course, it is more likely that the law of averages applies here, and the level of competence we experience in others is not so very far from our own.

The problem starts with understanding what we mean by really listening. For example, the human brain's default position is that it filters out huge amounts of information that comes to us via all of our senses, and hearing is no different. Our brains use 'mental maps', formed from our values and beliefs, our experiences and assumptions (including all our prejudices) in order to decide what we will attend to. Because what we can attend to is only a fraction of the information that comes at us every second. And this is not just when our colleague is complaining for the fifth time about the pot-holes in the A453, when we are obviously only half-listening. No, this is when we think we are paying attention. So listening well means going beyond this default position. It requires effort.

Furthermore, listening well requires more than just our ears. A better term would probably be *attending* because good listening requires us to pay attention to facial expressions, body language, in fact the whole person. It requires us to check our understanding sometimes and summarise what we think we understood. Above all, it requires us to do this without rushing to judgements or filling in the gaps with our own assumptions and preconceptions.

Finally, even if we make a real effort and attend to someone well, we may not be applying the right kind of listening. Yes, we can listen with different intentions, which may or may not be appropriate to the circumstances. Complicated, isn't it? Let's recap.

> » We are pre-programmed to listen selectively, under 'normal' conditions.

> » Good listening uses more than just our hearing.

> » We do not just have to listen well, we also have to listen appropriately.

What happens otherwise? Well, we've all experienced poor listening, both personally and on reality television shows. What we fail to find out from communication we tend to make up, this generally results in people working in the same team or organisation but pursuing very different realities. Ever spoken with a colleague or boss and felt like you were living in a parallel universe?

How can we recognise 'default' listening in ourselves or others? Here are some of the things that might be happening.

» **We wander** – we are distracted by the fat pigeon on the window sill or that spot on the end of the speaker's nose.

» **We avoid** – we ignore things that do not fit with our goals and interests.

» **We compete** – we try to think of something we have done that is better.

» **We compute** – we focus exclusively on getting the facts or numbers and ignore the story or feelings or ideas.

» **We rescue and solve** – we sympathise so much with other person that we just want to give them an answer or solution that makes life easier for them.

(Adapted from Pemberton, 2006)

So, what does really attending to the other person look like? This is often referred to as 'active listening'.

» **We demonstrate understanding** – looking, nodding, reinforcing, *I see*.

» **We avoid interrupting**.

» **We resist distractions** – focusing fully on what the other person is saying, listening for use of language, imagery, patterns and themes.

» **We avoid judging content or delivery** – learning to recognise our filters and temporarily disable them.

» **We maintain our attention** – maintaining eye contact, summarising occasionally and checking our understanding.

» **We allow silences** – resisting the urge to fill pauses, encouraging the other person to continue.

» **Listen between the words** – being receptive to what is not said and what feelings lie behind the words.

(Adapted from Baguley, 2002)

Here is a little experiment you might try. Ask someone to talk to you about an unresolved issue with which they are struggling, and just listen to them actively for five minutes only, following the guidelines above, but without interrupting, or sympathising, or telling them about you, or trying to give them a solution. Be warned. This takes a lot of effort. It will feel exhausting, certainly at first, and if it does not, then you are probably not doing it right. But learning to really listen well will pay off and get you noticed. See what feedback you get. The likelihood is people will not experience listening like this every day.

So far, so good. But what is all this stuff about appropriate listening? Well, much of our lives, as teachers, managers and parents, is about getting things done, solving problems and moving on. As a consequence, we often adopt what we might call a diagnostic approach to listening. In other words, we puzzle-solve, picking out facts and clues that will help us to piece together what we feel is the most effective solution to this particular problem. There is nothing wrong with this, so long as it is our problem to solve, or the person we are listening to is incapable of responding to the issue themselves. Where it becomes counter-productive is when we are trying to develop the other person's problem-solving ability and help them learn. Under these circumstances, then the filtering for hard facts and clues, the focus on listening for own benefit, and the lack of attention to the other person's intrinsic knowledge, their emotions or state of mind mean we miss the opportunity to develop their abilities and instead make them dependent upon us for solving their problems in future. That is not a helpful outcome.

So try this little exercise. Have a look through the various exchanges dotted throughout this book, and see where you can spot examples of really good, or really poor, listening. See if your answers match ours (below).

Good and bad listening

So what examples did you come up with? Here are ours:

GOOD: *Jason and Sarah are both pretty good listeners. Just look at Jason's conversation with Harry in **H is for HE in FE** (p 60), or Sarah's chat with Norman in **I is for Influencing** (p 67). They both use processes such as reflecting back to demonstrate that they have understood the emotions and concerns of the other person.*

BAD: *Well, our awards for bad listening have to go to Norman and Parveen. Just take a look at Norman interviewing in **S is for Selection** (p 137), his attempt at conflict management in **C is for Conflict** (p 32), or his conversation with Raj in **M is for Motivation** (p 107). Meanwhile, Parveen shows her uncanny ability to avoid what she doesn't want to hear in discussing Seating with Sheena (p 135), Employability issues with Harry (p 48), and again when attempting to mentor Harry in **M is for Mentoring** (p 98).*

M is for Managing Upwards

Harry and Angela, section leaders at Bogginbrook College of Further Education, have been having a bad week/month/year and are venting their spleen over a coffee in the 'Mega-Bites' snack bar.

HARRY: *Sorry, I can't be long. I seem to have just acquired another job. That's four now, I think, or is it five? Any idea what 'Benchmarking training standards' might involve?*

ANGELA: *No, but I'll bet it doesn't involve doing the job you're actually paid for. Remember when you had time to do that properly?*

HARRY: *I dunno, it's kind of flattering to be asked to do these things. It's just that I feel so dumped on. The senior team are under pressure about achievement rates and the private sector mob muscling in on skills training, so muggins here gets handed another exercise in self-justification, rather than having the chance to actually improve things.*

ANGELA: *Ah well, ours is not to question why, ours is but to lump it or go get a decently-paid job.*

HARRY: *They just don't know what they want. They adopt this knee-jerk response to every report or initiative that comes out of government without any sense of a long-term strategy or objectives. So I'm just going to end up buggering around from pillar to post, trying to get my hands on information that shows what a great job we're doing from people who won't give it to me because they're scared it might show the exact opposite!*

ANGELA: *You should just tell them where to shove their 'Benchmarking', and stick to what's on your job description.*

HARRY: *Well, I've got to admit, I did let Parveen have it a bit this time. Told her why it was so difficult. I've got no time. I'm snowed under with paperwork as it is. The people I need to talk to won't co-operate. The objectives aren't clear enough. And employers won't give a toss about the results anyway.*

ANGELA: *There you go! So why bother?*

HARRY: *Because I'll still get bollocked from here to kingdom come, if it's not done how they want ...*

If any of this sounds vaguely familiar, you are not alone. Not only in further education, but in all sorts of organisations throughout the world, managers experience the frustrations of feeling trapped between the competing demands of their customers/clients/learners and their teams and the senior managers they report to. If the sector or organisation is going through a lot of change (and what organisation isn't?) then the conflict and stress will be all the more acute.

This is often presented as exclusively a middle-management dilemma, but the truth is that teachers, managers and team leaders at all levels in a college have a 'boss' somewhere, whose priorities may not always appear consistent with their own or their team's. As a consequence, canteens, water-coolers and corridors everywhere ring to cries of *What the hell do they think they're doing?* and *I don't know what they want any more!* and *Why don't they ever listen to me?*, as virtually everyone in the organisation blames the mythical 'they' for all their anxieties and frustrations.

But, consider for a moment that our little vignette is also an illustration of how dis-empowering self-talk can keep us in the role of victim and convince us all that there is nothing to be done. Instead of focusing on the things we may like to complain about, what if we were to look at what it *is* in our power to change? Can we change our own behaviour to 'manage' relationships with our own bosses (and peer group) more effectively?

A helpful way into this is simply to think about what you might value in those who report to you. Here are some thoughts.

» **Take a coaching/mentoring approach** – particularly if you feel at odds with what is being proposed, try asking questions, listening and summarising to explore possible areas of compromise, or to improve mutual understanding. (Of course, if digging your trench, getting in and putting your tin hat on has ever actually worked for you, then by all means stick with that...) Master the art of disagreeing without being disagreeable.

» **Agree SMART objectives** – help your boss by suggesting ways of making objectives for a task/project more Specific, Measurable, Realistic and Time-bound (see **O is for Objectives**).

» **Take responsibility** – if things appear muddled, suggest an agenda. Be clear about what can be done, but be helpful, not obstructive.

» **Agree and forget** – what every boss wants. Once everything is clear and agreed, it will get done on time or you will go back and keep her posted. No one likes to be chased so don't give her a reason to do this.

» **No surprises** – none of us likes to be caught out, particularly in front of *our* boss. So get into the habit of regular informal communication with your manager to keep them informed of progress.

» **Talk solutions not problems** – instead of thinking of a hundred reasons why something cannot be done, try to go armed with alternatives.

» **Ask for help** – don't be afraid to admit what you don't know, but accompany this with a willingness to learn. We are all secretly flattered by requests to use our expertise and knowledge to help a colleague.

» **Ask for and respond positively to feedback** – your boss might not, so help him by modelling the behaviour of someone who believes in lifelong learning.

» **Build, maintain and use your networks** – you may actually have influence that your boss lacks in some quarters. You may have been around longer, or just forged stronger relationships with certain people. Can you help smooth the way?

» **Adapt your influencing style** – find what works best with different people, but remember that gaining and keeping rapport, asking questions, listening actively, summarising benefits and working towards a decision will always help.

This is not about being an inveterate boot-licker or senior management 'clone'. On the contrary, it is about taking control and choosing to act and be treated as a responsible adult who believes they can and should influence what is going on.

M is for Market

We are accustomed now to thinking of ourselves in FE as competitors in a market for post-compulsory education and training. This wasn't always the case. The Further and Higher Education Act (1992) marked a changing point in the provision of post-compulsory education. It was an enactment of the proposals set out in the 1991 **White Paper**, *Education and Training for the 21st Century*, one of the most far-reaching of which was that FE colleges (and also sixth form and tertiary colleges) were to be removed from the control of Local Authorities, then known as Local Education Authorities (LEAs). This transformation of FE colleges into corporate bodies became known as *incorporation* and marked the real beginning of a 'quasi-market' in FE, as colleges whose provision had previously been managed and agreed strategically under regulation by the LEAs began to operate as individual corporate organisations. Competition for students now sometimes began to involve offering courses and qualifications which duplicated provision in neighbouring colleges and sixth forms. The necessity to compete in a crowded market has created the current situation in which stronger (larger, better resourced, or more entrepreneurial) colleges thrive at the expense of others which have competed less successfully in the market. This inevitably led to some college closures and mergers. In addition, by encouraging schools to include vocational education in their post-16 curriculum with the introduction of General National Vocational Qualifications (GNVQs), the 1992 Act was also responsible for creating further competition between schools and colleges for attracting or retaining pupils at 16. In a number of ways, therefore, the Further and Higher Education Act of 1992 was responsible for pushing the tertiary sector of education firmly into the world of competition and market forces.

This has brought about fundamental changes to the nature of the professional's role in FE. The imperatives of the market, with its emphasis on competition and survival, are shifting the focus of management away from purely curriculum issues and increasingly towards concerns about funding, cost-effectiveness and statistical returns. This may make some roles more challenging and fulfilling, but it can have another consequence, too, which is a widening gap between the agenda of managers and those whom they manage. For colleagues in FE who are primarily teachers, the important agenda is naturally about pedagogic and curriculum issues, whilst the agenda of many managers is dominated – whether they like it or not – by financial and strategic demands. This apparent lack of a common agenda can lead to miscommunications and misunderstandings which require careful management to resolve. And for those managers who also retain a substantial teaching role – such as subject and team leaders – these competing agendas can be the cause of role conflict and stress if left unacknowledged and unaddressed.

However, we're looking here at competing agendas, but not necessarily at conflicting ones. Curriculum, pedagogy, targets and funding are all issues to be addressed in the interests of raising and sustaining a good quality of provision for the FE learner.

Further reading

For an interesting critique of market competition and its impact on services such as education and health, see:

Sandel, M.J. (2013) *What Money Can't Buy: The Moral Limits of Markets*. London: Penguin Books.

M is for Meetings

Norman has convened a meeting.

OK is everyone here? ... Angela's late as usual. I wonder if I told her it had changed from Room 6? ... Well, let's just start without her. She hasn't made the last three meetings anyway. OK folks. Sorry I didn't get the agenda out before, but I've got some copies here, if you'll just pass them round ... You might have to share ...

I don't think there's any matters arising. We didn't really come to any firm conclusions last time, I seem to remember, so perhaps we should just go round the table and see where we're each at on this one ... er, Harry ... Harry! ... Could we just have one meeting please ...?

Sound familiar? We probably all spend more time than we would like in apparently pointless and sometimes badly-run meetings which seem to go on for ever and achieve very little. So why not just ban them altogether (or avoid them, like Angela)?

Tempting, I know; but the truth is that meetings do serve a very important purpose, several in fact.

> » They help to define the team and establish collective identity.

> » They combine the knowledge, experience and creativity of the group to produce more powerful and cohesive decisions.

> » They create commitment and mobilise people into action.

> » They share information and improve communication.

Well, that's the theory, at least. What may actually happen is this:

> » as a result of galloping megalomania, or insecurity, or both, the chair-person just uses the group to rubber-stamp plans he/she has already decided upon;

> » the proceedings are entirely dominated by a few individuals who talk end-lessly and say very little. (When they're not in meetings, they sit next to you on the train and talk on their mobile phone.);

> » you all have an amusing/riveting/stultifying discussion for three hours, sometimes – if you're really lucky – followed by a rather pleasant lunch, and two days later no one can remember what was said.

Of course, we never run meetings like this, do we? No, because we follow a few simple guidelines.

A meeting? Are you sure?

» Don't have a meeting just because it's Thursday or the month end or your predecessor used to have one. Some meetings may be mandatory, but assuming you are calling the meeting, only have it if it will fulfil one of the purposes above, and even then, only if there is not a more effective way of achieving the same end.

Get yourself organised

» If it is your meeting, prepare an agenda, or some definite objectives for the meeting and circulate two or three days before. If it is not your meeting – for example, if representatives of employers or an examining body have requested a meeting at the college – it is reasonable to ask for and expect that they will provide you in good time with an agenda. (Tip: if no one can come up with objectives or an agenda, you could suggest that you don't need a meeting.)

» If you are putting the agenda together, order it logically (eg lively, creative activity early on).

» Try to keep topics covered to what can be achieved in a maximum of two hours.

» Be alert and sensitive to matters which may divide the group.

» Wherever possible, give people in advance any lengthy stuff that needs to be read; at the same time as you give them details of time, venue, etc. And then maybe even remind them when the meeting's about to come up, so that they remember to do the reading as well as attend.

» Sort out the seating arrangements, audio-visual kit, etc. in advance of the meeting.

Make the discussion count

What you're usually aiming to do as chair is:

» define the issue/problem;

» collect all available and relevant facts/opinions;

» generate alternatives before agreeing a diagnosis or solution;

» decide on a course of action.

Be a servant to the group and don't take sides

»   Listen (we often devalue this in meetings, accusing people of not making much of a contribution when they may simply be reflecting on matters).

»   Ensure all are motivated and involved, including the quiet ones, even if this means politely shutting others up.

»   Summarise all the way through, and check understanding.

»   Keep the group focused on objectives.

»   Make sure there is consensus and conclusions are reached, or further actions agreed. (If you have a lot of meetings without this happening, you may want to question what purpose they are serving.)

Nail it down

»   Finally summarise discussion and review against the objectives of the meeting.

»   Leave people feeling something has been achieved.

»   Remind people of actions, when they are required and from whom.

»   Never action someone not at the meeting (though this is always tempting.).

»   Never let the discussion ramble on once agreement is reached.

»   As a minimum, make sure a note is kept of time/date/location, who attended, a list of what was discussed, and actions agreed by name/date. When you come to put documentation together for the next Ofsted or QAA visit you'll be pleased to have nice, orderly records of all meetings held.

M is for Mentoring

Let's have a look at a recent meeting between mentor and mentee at Bogginbrook College. Parveen is Harry's mentor.

PARVEEN: *Hi Harry, come in. How are you feeling today?*

HARRY: *Er ... fine thanks.*

PARVEEN: *That's fantastic Harry. I'm so pleased we could have this time together. I thought it would be an opportunity for us to dialogue, and explore how you're settling in to the new job.*

HARRY: *Oh, great, really good. I'm enjoying it so far. Well, it's all a bit unfamiliar, you know, but no ...I'm good ...*

PARVEEN: *Great, cool. Let's unpick that a bit, shall we Harry?*

HARRY: *How do you mean?*

PARVEEN: *Well, it sounds as though something's troubling you, something you perhaps feel it's hard to talk about.*

HARRY: *No, not really. I just need to find my feet that's all. Get to know my way around. I suppose I'm still learning who everyone is.*

PARVEEN: *I understand. And how does that make you feel, Harry? A bit of a stranger? An outsider? Like you're lost?*

HARRY: *No, I hadn't really thought any of those things ... until now ...*

PARVEEN: *Good, because I want you to know how much we value you as a person, as well as a colleague. I want you to know, Harry, that you can be anything you want to be.*

HARRY: *Well, I just want to be a reasonably competent section leader at the minute.*

PARVEEN: *Great! So now we're starting to build goals. Say with me, 'I can overcome anything to reach my goals'. Come on, let's hold hands while we say it, and try to picture what you'll look like when you're a reasonably competent section leader.*

HARRY: *Is this some sort of initiation ceremony?*

PARVEEN: *Gosh Harry, that's an interesting comment. Why do you think you felt the need to say that?*

Oh dear. We have already tried to address some of the confusion around mentoring and coaching (see **C is for Coaching**). Hopefully we have convinced you that the skills and even the processes involved are very similar. So we do not intend to address the skills and processes of mentoring here. Rather, we want to look at what happens when the two are confused and applied poorly. What happens when we stray away from the secure and well-defined pathways of classroom practice, competencies and national standards, and into the dimly lit and litter-strewn alleyways of personal motivation and self-actualisation. Mentoring is being used in a wider and wider range of contexts, as people realise how effective it can be. But it can still all seem a bit 'new-age' and 'touchy-feely' to the uninitiated. Parveen, with her patronising self-help manual mind games, and evangelical desire to uncover some hidden psychosis that she can 'cure', is doing nothing to dispel this suspicion.

Mentoring is not psychotherapy, nor is it having an 'old stager' use their wisdom and experience to solve all your problems for you. An important feature of mentoring (and coaching) relationships is having clear boundaries. Acting as amateur counsellor and psychotherapist, or teaching someone under the guise of mentoring would both lie outside these boundaries.

As we have already said, a good mentor should use the same sort of skills as a coach, skills such as questioning, listening, summarising and reflecting, to help you to:

» successfully navigate key transitions, such as moving into teaching from another profession, or becoming a team leader or manager, or even taking retirement;

» deal with future personal and career growth and develop plans which reconcile both personal and professional needs;

» or maybe just act as an empathetic sounding board for you to wrestle with a tricky problem or decision.

(See also **F is for Feedback, I is for Interviews** and **L is for Listening**.)

In doing this, the mentor will most likely be responding exclusively to your agenda and stated learning needs, rather than any requirement of the institution or profession.

On the face of it, this all sounds hunky-dory, and indeed an examination of all the existing research on mentoring new teachers, conducted in 2009, confirmed a whole host of benefits accruing to the mentee, the mentor and the wider institution.

For the mentee

» Reduced feelings of isolation.

» Better adaptation to norms and expectations of institution and profession as a whole.

» Increased confidence and self-esteem.

» Professional growth.

» Improved behaviour and classroom management skills.

» Improved time-management.

» Improved self-reflection and problem-solving capacities.

» Gaining perspective on difficult experiences.

» Increasing morale and job satisfaction.

For the mentor

» Positive impact on personal and professional development.

» Improved ability to learn through self-reflection on own practice.

» Opportunity to talk to others about teaching and learning.

» New and improved teaching styles.

» Improved communication skills.

» Satisfaction and pride in helping others succeed.

» Enhanced career planning through identifying own priorities.

For the organisation

» Increased retention and stability.

» Staff getting to know each other better.

» Increased collaboration.

» More developed culture of professional development.

» More cost-effective training and development of staff.

(Hobson *et al.* 2009)

If only this were the whole story, however. The same group of researchers also found evidence of:

For the mentee

» Unavailability and insufficient support for mentee's emotional and psycho-logical well-being.

» Increased pressure and anxiety.

» Feeling bullied.

» Not being sufficiently challenged.

» Not given enough responsibility or freedom to innovate.

» A focus on technical skills development at the expense of broader self-directed learning skills, such as critical reflection.

For the mentor

> » Increased workload.
>
> » Feelings of insecurity, threat or inadequacy.
>
> » A sense of isolation.

For the organisation

> » Staff withdrawing from the training or even profession.
>
> » An increase in theory-practice dualism and poor application of theoretical concepts.
>
> » The promotion of conventional as opposed to innovative practices.
>
> » A lack of challenge and reform.

(Hobson *et al.* 2009)

It seems clear from these results that what the research was actually examining was a mix of both mentoring AND coaching relationships. Nevertheless, how do we ensure that in our college we maximise the benefits of such processes and minimise the dangers? Leaving aside the obvious matter of how well-trained and skilful the mentors are, in our view the answer comes down to three parameters.

1. Definition of the role.
2. The conditions for mentoring (and coaching).
3. The quality of the relationship.

Role definition

Broadly speaking, the United States has by and large developed mentoring along a sponsorship model, with 'proteges' (their preferred term for 'mentees') benefiting from the wise counsel of older and more experienced mentors. By contrast, mentoring in Europe has taken a more developmental route, in which the focus is on the mentee's agenda, and the emphasis is on mutual learning and helping the mentee to do things for themselves. We can summarise the characteristics of these as follows:

SPONSORSHIP MENTORING	DEVELOPMENTAL MENTORING
Power is with more senior, experienced and knowledgeable mentor	Mentor need not have greater experience or knowledge, only different. Power is 'parked'

SPONSORSHIP MENTORING	DEVELOPMENTAL MENTORING
Mentor's role is to provide protection and promotion, but also to impart skills and knowledge	Mentor's role is to support and encourage, but primarily to question and challenge mentee in order to help them generate their own insights
Little or no emphasis on learning to learn	Primary emphasis on learning to learn
More likely to result in dependency	More likely to result in autonomy and independent thinking
Mentee agenda subservient to that of organisation?	Mentee encouraged to challenge organisational norms and assumptions

Conditions for mentoring

The way we define the role of mentor will have a knock-on effect on the conditions for mentoring within the college. For example, treating mentoring as primarily a means of experienced teachers passing on technical expertise to new recruits is likely to result in a more formalised scheme. By contrast, a college may choose to interfere little in mentoring relationships, leaving such matters as setting up the relationship and driving it forwards squarely with the learner. Under these circumstances the development agenda will be largely or even entirely their own, and may or may not correspond to national standards. The mentor is not there to assess the learner, only to help them reflect and come to decisions. The conditions the college chooses to establish will impact significantly on the way mentoring works. See the table below:

CONDITIONS	ADVANTAGES	DISADVANTAGES
Completely informal	Responsibility with learner. Improved self-reliance and independent learning. Focus on mentee needs. Mentor more motivated.	Lack of overall purpose. Little or no training. Incompetent mentors. Poor support networks. No resources allocated. Some people excluded.
Benign formality	Good quality training. Allocation of time and resources. Continuing support for mentees and mentors. Reduced isolation and feelings of insecurity. Clear purpose for institution. Equal opportunity.	Some responsibility and intitiative removed from mentee.

CONDITIONS	ADVANTAGES	DISADVANTAGES
Institutional formality	Some or all of above, plus: Closer control of process, mentor allocation and learning agenda.	Less freedom to question and innovate. Less emphasis on personal growth and learning to learn. Equal access may suffer. Time allocation may be squeezed.
Voluntary	Better motivated partnerships Rapport built quickly. Encourages independence.	No control over pairings. Unequal participation. Common aims and standards very difficult.
Compulsory	Standard provision. Equal participation. Fair to all. More control of pairings.	Feelings of pressure and inadequacy more likely. Reinforces status quo.
Imposed standards	Common treatment and assessment for all. Learners know what to expect.	Learners sacrifice some or all of own agenda to blanket standards and targets. Learners less committed.
Mentor also expected to assess	Mentor can give detailed feedback to reinforce learning agenda. Mentee is challenged.	Trust in learning partnership undermined by suspicion and insecurity. Mentee may become reliant on feedback at expense of critical self-reflection.

Relationship quality

The price we must pay, it seems, for the privilege of closely controlling mentoring, imposing standard processes and agendas, and mistakenly conflating mentoring, coaching, assessment and instruction is often a weakening of the bond between mentor and mentee. And yet there is pretty compelling evidence that the quality of the mentoring relationship may actually be the single most critical factor in determining mentee attitudes towards job and career (Ragins *et al.*, 2000). Other research suggests that the same is true of coaching. This may be unavoidable for coaching in FE, in the context of a process inextricably bound up with observation, assessment and performance management. But is there not a case for differentiating mentoring more clearly and handling these relationships differently?

So, what about your college? To what extent is the overwhelming importance of relationship quality reflected in:

» The initial training given to mentors and mentees?

» The continuing development and supervision of mentors?

» The evaluation of the mentoring programme?

» The way mentors and mentees are matched?

» The additional demands made on mentors which may conflict with an open, trusting and non-judgemental relationship (eg assessment, line management, etc.)?

The best mentoring relationships are based on:

» TRUST and SUPPORT – in order to talk honestly about your experiences, feelings and development needs, you have to be sure that the person sitting opposite is prepared to suspend judgement, has your best interests at heart, and believes you are capable of learning and developing further. This is why mixing the role of immediate line manager and mentor can be tricky;

» RAPPORT – without this you are unlikely to be open about yourself or take on board feedback, however constructive;

» A CLEAR AGENDA – if the person being mentored (the 'mentee') cannot immediately identify the agenda themselves (and they may be seeking a mentor to help them do just that), they must be allowed to take the lead in developing and agreeing it, together with their mentor;

» DISCOVERY – mentoring works by helping someone arrive at their own learning through skilful questioning and listening, not by instruction or direction. As a mentor, you may well have relevant experience to share, but this is always secondary to encouraging the mentee to arrive at their own decisions. Where information or suggestions are appropriate, the mentor should earn permission to offer them. In an effective and supportive mentoring relationship mistakes can be embraced as an opportunity to learn;

» JOINT PROBLEM-SOLVING – like discovery, this challenges the *I know best, so do as I say* approach, and encourages a style based on pooling information, ideas and learning in a more collaborative way. Questioning and challenge from the mentee are seen as a prelude to learning and improvement, and not as an attempt to show you up and take over your job.

» OFF-LINE RELATIONSHIPS – given a limited cast of characters, all our mentors at Bogginbrook happen to be line managers of the people they mentor. In reality, this is not an ideal combination, and mentoring relationships are generally seen as more effective when they are off-line.

M is for Mission Statement

Are you familiar with your college's mission statement? Perhaps you had a hand in drafting or re-drafting it. The mission statement is a statement of intent against which college achievement may be measured. In other words, the college is as answerable for its mission statement as Captain Kirk was for his declared intent to boldly go where no one has gone before. Though life as an FE professional may sometimes seem like something out of science fiction, it's got to feel easy in comparison with that.

M is for Motivation

Raj goes to see Norman, his head of school, about a small group of learners who haven't handed in their work for assessment.

RAJ: *The thing is, Norman, they won't get their qualification if they don't complete this work and get it assessed.*

NORMAN: *Well, if that's not enough to motivate them, they don't deserve to get the qualification, do they?*

RAJ: *Come on, mate. Apart from what that attitude would do to our attainment figures and funding, it's not really fair on the learners, is it? They're only young. They don't think ahead. They don't always weigh up consequences. Obviously they don't feel motivated. So I have to find some way to change that.*

NORMAN: *Have you tried shouting at them?*

RAJ: *What?! Shouting at them? How's me raising my voice going to convince them that learning is an enjoyable experience? No, what I want to do is set up a system of rewards. Everyone who gets their work in on time gets extra time on the computers. And if everyone gets the work in on time, we have a team game for the last half hour.*

NORMAN: *Team game?*

RAJ: *Don't worry. It's a subject-related quiz. We have a league. They enjoy it. I've used it as a reward before.*

NORMAN: *Well, please yourself. I still think a good loud bit of shouting keeps them on their toes.*

RAJ: *Not half so well as praise and approval, Norman. Believe me.*

Psychologists tell us that there are two types of motivation: intrinsic and extrinsic. Intrinsic motivation is the drive that comes from within the individual themselves. They want to achieve; they want to succeed. They enjoy the process of learning and the sense of satisfaction that comes from having accomplished a task. Extrinsic motivation comes from outside, in the form of rewards or sanctions. A learner who won't hand in coursework on time for the simple satisfaction of doing so, might do it if they are rewarded with approval and praise, or a chocolate bar, or a deal that means they get more time on the computers next session. Or they might be prompted to hand in on time by the threat of a sanction, such as no computer time for a week.

It would be great if this was an ideal world and all our learners were intrinsically motivated. But it's not. And so, in reality, a large part of a teacher's role consists of finding ways to provide extrinsic motivation until learners reach a point where they recognise for themselves the satisfactions of learning and of a job well done. At that point their own intrinsic motivation kicks in. Norman is clearly of the view that sanctions work best, and that learners will hand in promptly to avoid being yelled at. Raj disagrees, and would rather provide some positive inducement. While Norman's method may work well in some contexts – the armed forces, for example – research, on the whole, supports Raj's approach.

(See also **B is for Behaviour Management** and **E is for Engagement 1**.)

N is for Negotiation

Zoe, a recently appointed team leader, ambushes her section head, Norman, over a coffee in the staffroom.

ZOE: *Norman, I've just heard Raj is being sent to the conference on self-assessment in London next month.*

NORMAN: *Well ... not exactly. He asked me a couple of months ago if he could attend, and I couldn't see any good reason why not, so ...*

ZOE: *So, how much money is left in our staff development budget then?*

NORMAN: *Oh, there's still quite a bit. Well ... when I say quite a bit, I mean, you know, there's some ...*

ZOE: *So why did you stop me going on that course on new curriculum requirements? I'm supposed to have special responsibility for that in this job.*

NORMAN: *Look, Zoe, you weren't section leader when you asked about that, and anyway it was in Edinburgh, and there's sure to be more of these sessions nearer home, which wouldn't cost so much.*

ZOE: *Haven't you got to spend that budget by next month, or risk a reduction next year?*

NORMAN: *Blimey, you have done your homework, haven't you? Be that as it may, there are other people with equally legitimate claims on these funds. I've got to be fair to everyone.*

ZOE: *So, who else's development requests are you considering?*

NORMAN: *Ah, well ... now ... it wouldn't really be fair of me to say ... Look, don't look at me like that. I've said no, and that's that.*

ZOE: *So, I have a genuine job need to attend this event, which is more than can be said for Raj. And it would improve my contribution to the whole curriculum debate hugely, but you're prepared to look as though you're discriminating against a female member of staff. Is it the hotel costs you're worried about?*

NORMAN: *Yes, that's exactly it. Edinburgh's incredibly expensive.*

ZOE: *Well, I've got family in Edinburgh. What if I stay with them? Then you've only got to cover the conference costs.*

NORMAN: *OK, I suppose that would be alright. Go ahead and book it, then.*

ZOE: *Great! Thanks. I'll have to fly up, because I'm teaching that afternoon ...*

We tend to see negotiation as a skill for managers, salespeople or buyers, but as this example shows, we can all of us find ourselves in what might loosely be called negotiations, whether informally, like this, or in a more formal context, over the timing of leave or the re-allocation of responsibilities, for example. Negotiation is the process of resolving conflict through compromise. By definition, this usually means both sides conceding something to the other. The final balance of concessions is what determines the success or otherwise of the discussion.

So what are some of the elements which affect the outcome of this encounter, and why is Norman so badly wrong-footed? Is this an example of a successful negotiation or not?

Let's look first at what you need to do to negotiate successfully.

Identify your objectives

» Be clear about exactly what you want to achieve from the discussion. Zoe had decided what she wanted. (And it looks as though a free visit to her family may have come into this somehow.) But Norman had no time to think what his objectives were.

» Try to divide the objectives into an ideal outcome, an acceptable outcome and a minimum fallback position. Have some idea before you start about what you can and cannot concede.

Identify key bargaining points

» These are the commitments you need to gain in order to move towards your overall objectives. In Zoe's case, she wanted to get Norman to admit that hotel costs were a key barrier. She also had a bargaining point about fairness, to do with her and Raj's relative needs.

Identify common ground

» Thinking about the other party's objectives as well as your own should enable you to identify where there may be common ground and where you may be able to extend it.

» You can then use this as a point to return to, if discussions get bogged down, or as a launch pad for a new proposal, counter-proposal, agreement, or adjournment. Zoe had spotted that spending the outstanding budget may be an area of common ground.

Ask questions

» Good negotiators ask twice as many questions, and listen hard. They want to find out information, rather than give it away. (You'll notice Norman asks only one question, and that's rhetorical.) Good general communication skills are vital to successful negotiation; not only questioning and listening, but summarising and checking understanding as well (see **I is for Interviews**).

» Use different sorts of questions to seek information, gain clarification and test for commitment.

Prepare your case

» Generally, people will shift their position in a negotiation if:

- they feel they have no option;

- remaining where they are will be unpleasant for them;

- they can see some real benefit in moving.

» So, prepare with these in mind:

- identify the strengths, facts which support your case, compelling arguments, previous custom and practice;

- think of the unpleasant consequences if your proposals are not agreed with (but be careful with this one. Norman sometimes doesn't get this right. See **B is for Bullying**);

- what are the benefits for everyone if they were to agree with your arguments?

(Can you see where Zoe made all three of these types of preparation?)

» In complicated or delicate cases, make notes.

- It's helpful to have an aide-memoire of the points you want to make, but stick to just a few powerful ones.

» Identify your weaknesses and/or the other party's strengths.

- Try to anticipate what arguments the other person may run and how you will respond.

Present your case

» Use common ground and key bargaining points to launch your case.

» Use your arguments to paint a compelling picture of what you want, and include the other party in it.

» But don't reveal all your points up front. Keep something in reserve.

» Follow some sort of structure.

- EXPLORING – questioning to gain information and test commitments. Listening to the other's case fully, without necessarily reacting. Making your case and agreeing an agenda of issues.

- EXPECTATION – use benefits and consequences of non-acceptance, but apply power gently at first, to avoid antagonising. Summarise arguments so far. Highlight common ground. Listen for signals of possible movement. Give signals of your own about where you may make concessions.

— MOVING – make realistic proposals and move only small amounts as necessary. Leave yourself room to manoeuvre. Let the other person make their proposals fully without interruption. Make any proposals conditional on concessions from the other party.

— CONCLUDING – is this the right moment, or is it too soon for the other person? Summarise any agreement in detail, with points of clarification and agreement.

So was Zoe and Norman's discussion a successful negotiation? That really depends on how you view the outcome. Did Zoe 'win' and Norman 'lose' (win–lose)? Did they both lose (lose-lose)? Or did they both win (win-win)?

We all know of situations, public or private, where the other side has been beaten into submission, or duped. However, the sign of a successful negotiation, especially informally within the team, is that relationships are maintained for the long term, and this means trying to achieve a win-win result. So, however shrewdly Zoe may have prepared and presented her case, if you think she has left Norman feeling mugged, then the negotiation was, to a degree, unsuccessful.

O is for Objectives

There are many aspects of our working lives, from appraisal and coaching to problem-solving, project management and lesson planning. How can we ensure that we establish and articulate these objectives as effectively as possible?

Let's look at an example. Here's Norman again:

What I want you to do, Angela, is see that our key local employer contacts are briefed about what's going on at the college. Make 'em feel kept in the loop. You know the sort of thing. Maybe a few sandwiches ... Oh, and a bit of a slide show, eh? Re-use my stuff from last time.

Is this a good quality piece of objective-setting? Clearly not, but this sort of thing is what passes for an objective amongst busy managers in many organisations. So how can we do better? You may have come across the following helpful acronym:

Specific	Clarify exactly what it is you want to happen.
Measurable	Ensure that you have some way of determining whether you have been successful in making this happen.
Agreed	Setting objectives generally involves more than one person. The most motivating objectives are those that we agree to voluntarily.
Realistic	To move us to action, objectives have to be achievable. They can be stretching, but they must be realistic.
Time-bound	When does this have to happen by? Failing other hard measures, most tasks can at least be assessed against an agreed deadline.

(Sometimes people add ER to the end of this, signifying the need for Evaluation and Review, making the acronym SMARTER.)

If we were to apply the SMART approach to our example, we'd perhaps get Sarah to brief Angela. Having discussed what is involved, the conclusion might look something like this:

OK Angela, so you're going to organise two similar events, on separate dates, when all local employers who are offering placements for learners will be invited to a briefing on the reorganisation. The purpose here is to send them away understanding who their new points of contact are and which course structures may alter. Both sessions need to have taken place before the end of April, and if they're successful we'll have briefed at least 75 per cent of the targeted employers and received a majority of good or excellent ratings on our event feedback sheets. Are you happy with all this?

Apart from conforming more to the requirements of the SMART model, two other characteristics distinguish this version from our first attempt. It has clearly been co-created as part of a two-way discussion between Angela and her boss, rather than issued as an instruction (even a rather vague one, like Norman's). So, if your boss is inclined to leave you with inadequate objectives, then use these tips to help her formulate better ones.

Second, although Angela is given a much clearer brief about what she must achieve, she is actually given greater freedom in how she goes about achieving it. Enabling people to act on their own initiative often means agreeing clear structures and standards that they can work to.

O is for Observations

Bogginbrook College is engaging in a self-assessment exercise prior to inspection. As part of this, the teaching staff are required to take part in peer assessments. Harry is going to observe Wayne. As this is Wayne's first year at the college Harry, as his line manager, has observed his teaching on two occasions already. But Wayne is still feeling nervous.

HARRY: *It's not bothered you before, though.*

WAYNE: *Yes it has. I just didn't let on.*

HARRY: *But it's no big deal. You're a good teacher. You've got nothing to worry about.*

WAYNE: *You're going to grade me this time. It's completely different. To be honest – and I know you're a good guy, Harry – but it feels like my whole* identity *is being judged. A teacher is who I am. It's part of who I am. And it's going to get* graded, *you know?*

HARRY: *Look, mate. It's part of the job. It's part of what we take on when decide to be teachers. Our performance gets graded every now and again. And it helps if you just think of it as one of the ways we keep up standards – one of the ways we keep the profession something to be proud of.*

WAYNE: *OK. But you know as well as I do that what you get to observe isn't what would be happening if you weren't there. Having an observer in the room changes everything. The learners behave differently. They get self-conscious. They get shy about contributing. Or else they act uncharacteristically compliant because they think that'll get me a good report. You'll* never *see what my lessons are really like.*

HARRY: *Well, we have to live with that, don't we? The alternative is secret cameras.*

WAYNE: *Parveen's probably had those put in already.*

HARRY: *Ssssh! In that case, there might be one in here.*

Feeling nervous is a quite natural response to being observed, even for excellent teachers and those with years of experience. Wayne's explanation – that so much of a good teacher's sense of self is invested in their professional identity – is an astute one. But also, any process that feels like a 'test' or presents the risk of failure is always guaranteed to cause some degree of anxiety. But there are things you can do to bring down the anxiety level.

Preparation

» Make sure you have a clear, detailed and realistic lesson plan and give your observer a copy.

» Make it clear how this lesson plan fits into the overall scheme of work and contributes to it.

» If there are learners in the group who have specific characteristics or learning needs which have informed your planning, make sure the observer has a note of this.

» Make sure it incorporates a plan B. In other words, if something you've planned misfires in some way, or a piece of IT kit fails to function, you have an alternative activity or resource to fall back on.

» Check out the resources and accommodation beforehand. Will the activities you've planned work in this room and with this equipment, or do you need to do some re-planning? Do you need to be there early to re-arrange seating? Is this feasible, given your timetable?

Observation

» Be enthusiastic. Smile. This will send signals to your brain that everything's OK.

» Don't do something completely different or out of character from your normal teaching. The learners will pick up on this and probably pass comment.

» If you worry that the presence of the observer will affect the behaviour of the learners or prove a barrier to their learning, set out a seat for the observer at the back of the room or in some other position away from the learners' eye-line.

» If you are concerned that having the observer permanently in sight will have an adverse effect on your confidence or your concentration, offer them a seat somewhere not directly in front of you.

(Hopefully these last two aims can both be achieved without having to actually seat the observer in a cupboard.)

Afterwards

» When you listen to the observer's feedback, pay careful attention to all of it – don't just focus on the grade. If you hear that there's room for improvement, try not to be defensive. Hearing an observer's view of your lesson can be very revealing, and you may learn something useful.

If you're the one doing the observing, you'll find it useful to bear all this mind and also to read carefully **F is for Feedback**.

P is for Paperwork

Question: What do you call someone who's standing up to their neck in paperwork?
Answer: A professional in FE.

Paperwork seems a quaint term in these electronic times. But whether the forms and returns and reports and audits and evaluations and all the rest are steadily accumulating in your e-mail inbox or in a wire tray, the effect is the same: paperwork clamours for your attention, whatever else you're doing.

To deal with it, you'll need to draw on a range of skills, most of which you'll find in this A–Z. They include:

> » **Time Management**: making considered judgements about what can or can't wait; for example, whether externally generated paperwork (eg from awarding bodies or Ofsted) should always be treated as more urgent than internal forms or responses. Paperwork is never finished. You can never cross that final return off the 'to do' list and sit back with a contented sigh. Managers who've come to terms with this fact and have organised their time to shift as much as they can, when they can, are happier managers.

> » **Delegation**: but don't forget that colleagues are most likely to be already inundated with paperwork of their own. The trick here is to use individual knowledge and expertise within the team while avoiding log-jams by not always overloading the same people. There may also occasionally be the opportunity to delegate upwards.

Perhaps the most important piece of accumulated wisdom, gleaned from all the FE professionals we've spoken to, is:

Never try to solve a problem by just creating more paperwork. There may be another way.

P is for Performance Management

For any line manager in FE, a perennial problem is how to meet constantly changing curriculum demands (such as working to revised assessment criteria or teaching 14–16-year-olds) while at the same time helping colleagues to develop their skills and career prospects; how to deploy staff to achieve organisational goals, while also encouraging them to develop to their full potential. A formal system of performance review is central to this key management task (see **A is for Annual Review/ Appraisal**). But what happens when we find ourselves dealing with staff who we know are performing badly? How do we manage poor performance?

As we suggest in the section on **As is for Annual Review/Appraisal**, a formal performance discussion once a year, however cleverly designed, will never have much impact. Formal review or appraisal works best when it is integrated into a wider framework of performance management. We tend to feel motivated when we experience a sense of purpose, achievement and recognition. So effective managers should ask themselves:

Sense of purpose

>> Do I understand what I and my team are really here for?

>> How do we contribute to the overall aims of the college?

>> What are the key result areas that make up this contribution?

>> How are they measured?

>> Do I regularly communicate all this to my team and ensure they understand it?

Achievement

>> What are the agreed standards to which I and my team should perform?

>> What are the measurable targets we have agreed to meet?

>> How am I ensuring that my team contribute to these, and remain committed to them?

>> Do I set a good example for others to follow?

>> How am I ensuring that individuals are stretched to fulfil their potential?

Recognition

» When did I last praise a member of my team for doing something well?

» Was I specific and did I give an example?

» Am I confronting unacceptable behaviour/performance promptly?

» Was I specific and did I give an example? Did I offer to help?

Internal quality systems such as self-assessment, and external inspection (for example by Ofsted and QAA) are often means of identifying areas of excellence in most colleges. Unfortunately, these same processes can occasionally result in the identification of staff who are judged to be 'failing'. Most managers in an FE college, and certainly most of the people working within a particular section, are well aware of who the 'good' teachers are and – if there are any – who are not. There is usually a wide variety of sources which provide informal feedback on individual performance. These may include student comment, letters of complaint, attendance and retention figures, peer observation, achievement figures or exam results and so on. In discovering that one of your team is under-performing or perhaps even struggling, you, as manager, have several options. You can:

» do nothing, in the hope that the problem will go away – usually a false hope, and sometimes a coward's way out of a possibly awkward confrontation;

» seek improvement by enlisting staff development resources;

» consider transferring the member of staff to other work which might allow them to play to their strengths;

» as a final resort, use the **disciplinary** process, recognising that a possible final outcome could be dismissal of the colleague involved.

To establish whether what you're dealing with can formally be identified as poor performance, you will need to look at the evidence. Weightman (1999) identifies a number of specific steps you might take as part of this process.

» Establish what criteria should be met in order for a performance to qualify as satisfactory.

» Gather reliable and current information about actual performance.

» Identify whether the gap between required and actual performance is such as to merit intervention.

» Determine the reason for the gap.

» Plan a course of action to deal with the problem.

There is no cure-all for poor performance, for the simple reason that it can arise from such a broad range of causes, from ill-health to inadequate professional development. As a manager, you have a number of strategies at your disposal for addressing poor performance in your team, most of which are listed in this A–Z. They include **A is for Annual Review/Appraisal**, **F is for Feedback**, continuing professional development (CPD) and – as an extreme measure – the **D is for Disciplinary** procedure.

P is for Politics

Parveen, head of health and social care, is e-mailing Norman, head of travel and tourism. She has copied in Sarah, head of faculty and Norman's boss.

Norman,

Thanks for your recent note, requesting that I find some way of releasing Harry from his Wednesday afternoon classes to attend your Basic Skills working party. I was surprised that you had spoken to Harry about the possibility of joining this, without consulting with me first.

I'm sure you will appreciate that my school, with its excellent Ofsted grading, is currently under a lot of pressure from the principal and corporation to increase student numbers, particularly as areas like your own are suffering a bit of a retention struggle at present. I am, as we speak, trying to persuade the college to increase my school staffing budget in order to accommodate this planned expansion.

Obviously, I do not wish to deprive Harry of the opportunity to participate in a cross-faculty team, or prevent you from delivering such a high-profile project. However, without additional resources, I find it difficult to see how I might justify agreeing to your request.

Yours,

Parveen

Ouch! Is this what we mean by being 'political'? Parveen is certainly displaying many of the 'games' of a seasoned operator here: building territory and consolidating her powerbase, whilst undermining her competitor in the resources stakes and dropping him in it with his boss, to boot. Our lingering sense (and probably Norman's) is that she must have more than her stated agenda in mind.

So do you wholeheartedly embrace a political perspective on organisations, as communities, like any other, racked with divisions between different interest groups, all fighting for position, power and resources? Or do you see politics as a destructive by-product of any organised group, which is to be confronted and overcome by virtuous managers in the interests of everyone? Either way, there is no doubt that organisations, and certainly organisations as large and diverse as most colleges, cannot entirely avoid internal politics.

After all, colleges are made up of people, with different values and opinions, perhaps conflicting priorities and goals, and numerous informal alliances, all trying to use limited resources, hopefully to do the best job they can for the students. If we see 'politics' as, on the one hand, people finding ways to exercise power and influence, and, on the other, differences of interests, priorities or opinion leading to conflict, then 'politics' are neither avoidable nor necessarily a bad thing.

Whether as managers or team members, we may find ourselves having to navigate these priorities and vested interests in order to create some sort of order in this environment. It is the choices we make about how to do this that will determine the degree of conflict and whether it has a negative or positive impact. Politics and conflict can be an insidious distraction, preventing productive work. But conflict can also be a force for innovation, performance improvement and change. So this is something of a trade-off. How can we balance common goals and consensus with questioning and diversity in order to harness conflict more effectively, turning destructive back-stabbing into fruitful debate?

First we must study our own motives. Are we looking for constructive challenge or Yes people? A solution or a victory? Do we believe in striving for a win–win outcome? (See **N is for Negotiation**.) Is Parveen seeking a joint solution with Norman, or simply defending her patch? Are our own or our team's best interests served by competition and a struggle for control or by collaboration in helping each other achieve a mutually acceptable outcome?

Our approach will partly be determined by the conditions created in the college. Collaboration will be encouraged by:

- » having clarity around roles and responsibilities;
- » sparing use of rules and procedures;
- » a physical layout which discourages territorial instincts;
- » systems which facilitate sharing of information;
- » performance measures which are common and fair;
- » a trusting environment where mistakes are tolerated;
- » team goals which are aligned with a shared vision for the whole organisation (see **T is for Taking Responsibility**).

Think about what opportunities your own team gets to interact. People isolated on different sites, with little opportunity for face-to-face communication with colleagues, will easily invent hidden agendas and conspiracy theories to fill in gaps in their information. Generally, if the conditions are right, our behaviour towards colleagues is likely to be more constructive. But a college may even consider having explicit shared values and ground rules governing how individuals behave towards each other, to ensure that conflict is positively channelled. This could form part of the culture of **respect**. Here are some thoughts to get started.

>> Criticise ideas, not individuals.

>> Don't accuse people who are not there to answer.

>> Focus on team goals.

>> Be prepared to learn.

>> Ask questions and listen.

>> Help others contribute.

>> Clarify understanding and seek solutions instead of getting defensive.

>> Use appropriate communication (eg don't send an e-mail if it's a sensitive matter. Talk to them).

>> Demonstrate mutual respect.

>> Observe common social courtesies (eg greet and ask after people).

>> Avoid favouritism.

Further reading

You can read more about organisational politics in:

Handy, C. (1999) *Understanding Organisations*. London: Penguin.

Hatch, M.J. (1997) *Organization Theory*. Oxford: Oxford University Press.

Morgan, G. (1998) *Images of Organization*. Thousand Oaks: Sage.

More about constructive team-working can be found in:

West, M.A. (2004) *Effective Teamworking*. Oxford: BPS & Blackwell Publishing Ltd.

P is for Professionalism

NORMAN: *Have you got that marking finished yet, Angela?*

ANGELA: *Nearly.*

NORMAN: *You said that five weeks ago. Those learners have started their next assignment. They need the feedback from this one so that they know how they're doing and where they have to improve. It's a matter of* professionalism, *Angela.*

In the context of FE teaching, professionalism is demonstrated in two ways. One is by adherence to an accepted *code of practice* – much of which is embedded in college rules and policies and in the set of professional standards currently applied. This aspect of professionalism is about practices such as careful and appropriate lesson planning; ensuring coursework is marked promptly and rigorously; supporting learning effectively through the choice of appropriate strategies and the strategic use of differentiation; the duty of care to learners and colleagues; treating others with respect; and so on. These indicators of professionalism can be observed and assessed – and indeed they often are, during initial teacher training, college self-assessments and inspections. The other aspect of professionalism is, on the surface, less tangible. It is about holding and applying a *set of values*. It is about attitudes and beliefs, and is part of our internalised ethical guidance system. It's sometimes referred to as our *moral compass*. It is not reducible to competences which can be observed and assessed.

And yet the two are clearly and closely linked. You may not consciously think much about them, but your own professional values are what tell you that the externally applied codes of practice make sense. The two will converge. If they don't, you're probably in the wrong business.

To identify your own values and beliefs about being a teacher, here are some questions you can ask yourself:

> » Why do I want to be a teacher in FE?
>
> » What do I believe is the purpose of education and training?
>
> » What are my beliefs about the role of the teacher in the learning process?
>
> » What do I see as my responsibility, and where are its limits?
>
> » What do I understand as 'good' teaching?
>
> » Where does my greatest job satisfaction lie?
>
> » How do I demonstrate respect for a) my learners and b) my colleagues?

Q is for Quality

This is a word we hear a great deal in FE. We operate increasingly in a consumer culture in which education and training provision is required to meet standards of quality demanded by the 'customer' (see **M is for Market**). At the same time we are required to function within budgetary constraints. 'Quality', however, is rather a slippery term. It used to be associated with rank and luxury (remember the ladies and gents on those tins of Quality Street?) but in most organisations today, quality is measured by the level to which a product or service meets the needs of the customer. In terms of Total Quality Management (TQM) this is sometimes referred to as fitness for purpose. Applying TQM to college provision gives us three criteria for deciding whether an aspect of provision is achieving good 'quality'. These are:

» whether it does the job that it was intended to do;

» whether it's cost-effective;

» whether it can be easily accessed.

In other words, quality is defined by the requirements of our 'users' and clients, rather than by the college itself. There are some difficulties, as you'll see at once, in taking these definitions which originally related to a profit-making commercial context and applying them to an education and training organisation. What, for example, do we mean when we ask: *Does the provision do the job it was meant to do?* Are we talking about outcomes? Learner satisfaction? Employer satisfaction? Qualification rates? Progression rates? All of these? What job exactly is our provision meant to do? Defining quality outcomes in an FE context is not as straightforward as defining quality outcomes in a shoe factory; not least because it is often unclear whom we should regard as the end user. Is it the learner? The learner's employer? The UK economy? In some sense it's all of these and others, too.

Most of the time, however, we are saved from this philosophical debate by the use of Performance Indicators (PIs), Inspection Frameworks, and the quality frameworks of awarding bodies. And in most colleges, we now have a quality manager whose role is to co-ordinate, monitor and manage quality assurance across all aspects of the college's provision. Your own responsibilities may include the monitoring and assessment of quality, which may take a variety of forms, from the gathering of retention and achievement data to the observation of individuals' practical teaching.

R is for Recruitment

Contributing to decisions about recruitment and appointment is one of the most important jobs that a professional in FE has to do, even though at times this may seem like just a peripheral part of your role. Staffing is by far the largest element of college budgets, and therefore appointment of the wrong person can be an expensive mistake.

Recruitment and selection are part of the process of integrating the human resource requirement into the college's overall plans and objectives. This requirement is encapsulated in the college's long-term plan, which is then translated at faculty, department or school level to a faculty/department/school plan. This has to attempt the difficult task of forecasting the future size and shape of the curriculum, in three or five years' time, perhaps; and from this the ideal staff profile can be defined. This can be described as strategic human resource planning.

One of the first tasks for a line manager wishing to recruit new staff is to justify the appointment to senior management. For example, let's look at Sarah who, as head of sports and leisure studies, is deciding what to do about a vacant post for a lecturer in travel and tourism. The current post-holder is about to move on to a senior post elsewhere, having worked in the department for ten years on a wide range of programmes, from adult basic skills to HNC, and has acted as placement co-ordinator across all programmes. Sarah now has to choose which of the following options she should go for.

» Ask for a full-time replacement using the same job description.

» Re-allocate the work among existing staff and save the salary.

» Re-organise the job description and ask for additional staff in another curriculum area.

» Recruit part-time staff to cover her work.

Whichever choice Sarah makes, she'll have to justify her recommendation to senior management in terms of cost-effectiveness, student recruitment and strategic planning. The process may involve a job analysis, the outcome of which is the production of a job description or specification. Then the next step is to define the type of person who will best fit this job – this is the person specification. This will typically contain details of essential and desirable qualifications and experience, together with personal qualities and aptitudes.

The job and person specifications will form the basis for drafting an appropriate advertisement for a job. After application letters are received, the selection process begins. This almost always includes an interview (see **I is for Interviews**), perhaps in conjunction with some other method such as psychometric testing, a presentation, a 'live' teaching session, or a simulated task associated with the job. To find out more about selection interview techniques, see **S is for Selection**.

In having some input in the recruitment of your team, you will be contributing to decisions which will affect your working life as a manager perhaps for many years.

R is for Reflective Practice

Madge is required to keep a reflective journal as part of her initial teacher training. She's not quite sure what this involves, so she goes to see her mentor, Zoe, to ask her about it.

ZOE: *No, Madge, obviously you can't write down everything that happens every day. The purpose of a reflective journal is that it allows you to capture* critical incidents *so that you can reflect on them and learn from them.*

MADGE: *What does that mean, though, critical incident?*

ZOE: *Something significant. Something that stands out in your mind at the end of the day. Something you don't quite understand, maybe. Like, the learners may have really enjoyed the lesson and you want to have a think about what it was exactly that got them fired up. Or some activity may have worked really well with one group but been a complete flop with another, so you want to reflect on that and try to work out why. Or you may have had an interesting conversation with a colleague that's give you an insight into something that's happened in your own teaching. Anything like that.*

MADGE: *Oh right! I get it!*

ZOE: *But it's not just about thinking things out. It's also about using that to plan future action. So, for example, if you've noticed that a group concentrates really well in a lesson and you realise, on reflection, that it was probably because you'd set them a series of timed tasks to do, you'll use your understanding of that – the fact that short timed tasks work well – when you come to plan the next lesson.*

MADGE: *Thanks, Zoe. When I've written a bit up, will you read it through so you can tell me whether I'm being reflective enough?*

Zoe probably will. Madge is lucky to have such a hands-on mentor. If you have not been quite so fortunate, don't despair. You can check for yourself whether you are writing reflectively. There's a clear difference between reflective writing and descriptive writing. Descriptive writing records what happened. It's like a seaside postcard (*Went swimming today. Shark ate my snorkel*) or a ship's log (*Wind brisk from the S.E. Ship's cook burnt the porridge*). Reflective writing goes beyond the 'what' to explore the 'why' and the 'what am I going to do as a result.' In the context of a teacher's reflective journal it will follow a pattern something like this:

1. What went well today (or badly)?

2. Why or how did things happen this way?

3. What have I learnt from this about myself/my learners/my college/my mentor?

4. How can I usefully incorporate this understanding into my future practice?

5. How will this contribute to my action plan?

Zoe makes the point that genuine reflective practice involves planning future action in the light of experience. Simply thinking or writing about that experience is not enough. In this respect, reflective practice is closely linked to the type of inquiry known as *educational action research*. Here, a teacher identifies an issue they wish to address (for example, it might be a small group of learners in a class who never contribute to group discussions); the teacher tries out a strategy or *intervention* aimed at addressing this; and then reflects on what happened in order to evaluate whether this strategy has made a difference. If it hasn't, they may go on to try further *interventions* until they find something that works. This process or cycle of reflection–action–reflection is usually recorded in a reflective journal.

You should never think of reflective journals, therefore, as simply a hoop that trainee teachers have to jump through. They are a central and essential part of many teachers' professional practice, as well as being a recognised tool for academic research.

R is for Resilience

Ever noticed how some people seem to glide through life with a smile on their face, resolutely upbeat about the gifts life has showered on them in the past, the fun they are having now and their prospects for the future? How they seem to bounce back from adversity, dust themselves off and start all over again with renewed energy and vigour? Don't you just hate them?

Actually, you most probably do not hate them. In fact you most probably *are* one of them. Because the research seems to suggest that more of us are natural optimists than pessimists. If you are not one of life's optimists (and maybe even if you are), you could be forgiven at times for seeing the relentless promotion of positive thinking in recent years as a new form of semi-religious orthodoxy, under which anyone who does not *give 120 per cent* or *just goes for it* or sets out to *beat their terminal illness* is somehow just not trying hard enough. It is true that research shows a positive outlook can improve general health and recovery rates from some illness. Also, joking aside, most of us probably prefer to be around positive people than moaning minnies. But the truth is not all of us can be sunny optimists, and the world would be a more dangerous place without the odd pessimist to point out what might go horribly wrong with that great idea for driverless cars or re-mortgaging your house to finance your new knitted swimwear business.

Most of us can probably improve our ability to cope with setbacks, however, and whichever end of the optimism/pessimism scale you veer towards, the factors which help you cope with difficulties, the conditions which determine your ability to withstand stress, conflict and the other inevitable frustrations and disappointments of your life, seem to be much the same.

Back in 1989, Ryff proposed six conditions for psychological well-being.

1. Autonomy – we feel better when we are able to make our own decisions about our lives and work.

2. Environmental mastery – we feel better when we have a sense of control over our environment.

3. Personal growth – we feel better if we are developing and learning new things.

4. Positive relations – we feel better if we have people around us whom we love and who love us in return.

5. Purpose – we feel better if we are clear about what we want from work and life, if our existence has some meaning for us.

6. Self-acceptance – we feel better if we are comfortable in our own skin and accept ourselves for who we are.

Great, you may be thinking, *chance would be a fine thing. If only my average working day had half of these things. Tell all that to my boss. Lucky if I have the autonomy to use the photocopier without a chit from someone or other ... etc. ... etc..*

And it is true that there are people and circumstances in our lives which we cannot control. Nevertheless, look at that list again and ask yourself whether you could:

» do more to focus your energies on what is within your control?

» do more to learn new things and develop yourself personally or professionally?

» do more to build and maintain strong relationships with those around you?

» do more to connect with what your true purpose in life is and what is most important to you?

» do more to appreciate your strengths and achievements, and take on board positive feedback from others?

Furthermore, we *do* have control over the way we *respond* to negative events, This is the aspect of our behaviour that positive psychology has focused on for some years now, and one of the leading academics in the field, Martin Seligman, has identified a number of simple ways we can teach ourselves to be more positive and therefore more resilient. Here are some of them:

ABC – Adversity Beliefs Consequences

» C (emotional consequences) do not stem from A (the adversity itself) but from B (your beliefs or assumptions about the adversity). Learn to separate these and challenge your negative assumptions.

Identifying 'Icebergs'

» Can you recognise in yourself deeply-held beliefs that may lead to unhelpful reactions (eg asking for help is a sign of weakness).

Minimising catastrophic thinking

» If faced with automatically fearing the worst, try to replace with worst case, best case, most likely case.

What went well (three blessings)

» Each night for a week use a journal to record three things (big or small) that went well today and *WHY* they happened (Yes, your mum was right. You *should* count your blessings.).

Every organisation, your college included, needs both the realism and critical thinking to see the obstacles ahead, and the hope and perseverance to overcome them successfully. At a personal level, though, it is when you are faced with setbacks and challenges that a more positive outlook may help to strengthen your resilience and produce a better outcome.

Further reading

You can read more about resilience in:

Ellis, A. (1999) *How to Make Yourself Happy*. Atascadero: Impact Publishers.

Seligman, M. (2011) *Flourish*. London: Nicholas Brealey Publishing.

R is for Respect

NORMAN: *Shut up, you. I've no time to listen to your rubbish. Clear off. You're blocking my light.*

LEARNER: *Sorry, but I ...*

NORMAN: *Shut up. Clear off. And learn some respect.*

There are two senses in which respect is a key issue for any teacher or manager in FE. The first, which is about carrying out your role in such a way as to earn the respect of learners and colleagues, we deal with in some detail under **A is for Authenticity**, **E is for Emotional Intelligence** and **L is for Leadership**. The other sense in which respect becomes part of your remit as an FE professional is to be found in the phrase *culture of respect*. This is an expression increasingly in use in political discourse about education; and in many colleges it has become translated into a policy of respect which sets out for the benefit of staff and learners the rules governing acceptable behaviour on the college premises. This may involve such regulations as: no mobile phone use during lessons; no smoking except in designated areas; no use of offensive language on college premises; and so on. Whether your college refers to it in such terms or not, there will certainly be a conduct policy or set of rules of some kind which it is your responsibility to uphold and enforce. The respect agenda in colleges is often used to encompass and address a number of important issues. One of these is, of course **behaviour**, including professional and social interactions both inside and outside the classroom. Another is **diversity** and the need to ensure that no group or individual is bullied, disadvantaged or alienated because of their perceived 'difference'. A third is social and environmental responsibility, which may include anything from keeping the college campus free of litter to recycling and the responsible use of resources such as paper and electricity.

Whatever their specialist subject or vocational area, all teachers also have a responsibility to teach respect. The most effective way to do this is by modelling good practice. Behaving with respect towards our learners, our colleagues and our environment will always work better than simply talking about it.

In dealing with difficult situations you may find the following guidelines useful.

>   » **Always model the behaviour you expect to see**. For example, avoid such commands as: *Don't f***ing swear at me!* And if there's a no phones, no smoking policy, don't light up and phone home until you're off the premises.

» **Avoid confrontation and escalation**. If you need to reprimand a learner, choose your moment and remember that even in this aspect of your role you should still be aiming to provide a model of reasonable and civilised (albeit firm and authoritative) behaviour.

» **Know when to turn a blind eye**. Chasing up every minor misdemeanour will not only leave you no time for anything else, but will also devalue the effectiveness of your wrath or disapproval. It's about having a sense of scale, and making sure your team shares the same realistic set of priorities; so that if any of you are going to really read the riot act, you save it for something serious like bullying, rather than a minor infringement of dress code. This doesn't mean, however, that you should decide for yourself which rules count. Rules are rules, and as a professional it's your responsibility to uphold them (see **Z is for Zero-Tolerance**).

» **Be fair, and be seen to be fair**. This is one of the best ways to foster a culture of respect.

» **Behave towards others with respect**, whatever their status. This is the most effective way to gain respect for yourself. (Norman, it seems, hasn't quite got the hang of this one.)

S is for Seating

Parveen catches Sheena in the car park early in the morning to talk to her about class-room layout.

PARVEEN: *You were the last one in C25 yesterday?*

SHEENA: *I ... yes, I guess so. The twilight slot. I was in there 5:30 to 8:30.*

PARVEEN: *And you left it in a shambles.*

SHEENA: *Excuse me?*

PARVEEN: *You left the tables in a non-standard configuration. The cleaners have complained.*

SHEENA: *A non-standard ...? Oh, you mean I moved the tables into a horseshoe shape. Yes, that's right. It was an adult evening class. The tables are set out in four groups normally. It just doesn't work. People end up sitting with their backs to one another, or to me. We can't all make eye-contact. Whole-group discussion is very difficult, and people tend to only get to know the people they're sitting with. So we shifted the tables to make a big horseshoe shape so we could all see one another. It was much better for the group dynamic.*

PARVEEN: *Well, don't do it again.*

SHEENA: *I'm sorry, but I shall be doing it again, Parveen. Because it's in the best interests of the learners. But I'll make sure it's all moved back into – what was it? – the* standard con-figuration *before I leave.*

Seating arrangements can be of crucial importance to effective learning. Sheena explains here several of the reasons why this is so. While small groups at separate tables can be very useful for groupwork tasks and small group discussion, it's an arrangement which can be counter-productive when it comes to whole group communication. As a teacher, you will find it more difficult to gain the attention of learners who are seated facing away from you. Learners themselves will not be able to communicate effectively with each other outside their small group. Some will not be able to see the screen or board without moving their seat. This arrangement also lends itself to the formation of cliques and various forms of segregation. It allows learners to 'opt out' or disengage, and can facilitate social isolation or bullying.

As teacher, you are responsible for managing the immediate teaching environment. This includes seating arrangements. If the tables are in rows and you think that's likely to make the learners feel as though they're in an exam or back at school, re-arrange them. And then, hopefully with the learners' help, put them back where they were afterwards. There may well be rules about a standard configuration, but that's likely to be for practical reasons such as ease of cleaning rather than for pedagogic ones. The exception to this, of course, is when it's a matter of health and safety and the risk of blocking fire exits, etc.; in which case you simply have to put up with it. (I bet Parveen wishes she'd thought of that one.)

S is for Selection

Norman is head of the department of travel and tourism. Selecting a new departmental admin assistant has not been top of his priority list, but a series of disastrous temps has forced him to put aside some time and do some interviews. For him, as for many of us, this is only an occasional duty, and for that reason, feels rather unfamiliar.

NORMAN: *Are you here for the interview?*

OLIVIER: *Yes, I'm not sure if ...*

NORMAN: *Great stuff. Let's just see if this room's being used. Doesn't look like it. Don't worry about the noise. The sheet-metal work class finishes at three. Have a seat.*

OLIVIER: *I wasn't sure if this was the right place. The lady on the phone wasn't too specific.*

NORMAN: *Mmm ... Good, good ... Sorry, I'm just reading your CV ... You don't seem to have stayed in jobs very long. Why is that? Do you find it hard to settle, or do you just get bored easily?*

OLIVIER: *Well, neither really. My wife is a retail manager and used to get moved around from branch to branch. But now she's in a head office job.*

NORMAN: *Following your wife around, eh? That must stick in the craw a bit?*

OLIVIER: *It was frustrating sometimes, but she is the major breadwinner, and my job allows me to work more flexible hours and look after the kids.*

NORMAN: *But you don't mind all that, and being an admin assistant, even though you're a bloke? Is it a French thing? You are French, I take it?*

OLIVIER: *My mother is French, and no, I enjoy my work. I'm expert at all the basic Office applications, good with people and I'm well-organised.*

NORMAN: *I've just noticed here it says you were in the army.*

OLIVIER: *Yes, for three years, before I was married. I worked mainly in Stores and Logistics for the Royal Engineers.*

NORMAN: *Good for you, son. Best training you can get. Ah, here's Personnel, at last. I think we've found our man, Simon ...*

You may have spotted a few unconventional aspects to Norman's selection interviewing style. You may even have run into him yourself (or wanted to). Having looked earlier at some of the generic skills of interviewing, use this section to remind yourself of the specific issues around reaching selection decisions. We have divided this into:

» Preparation

» Structure

» Questioning

>> Recording

>> Pitfalls

Preparation

As Norman ably demonstrates, preparation can make the difference between an effective and highly professional job and car-crash management. First of all, before any selection takes place, a job description for the vacant role and an agreed person specification should be drawn up (see **R is for Recruitment**). This can be used to determine which criteria (eg experience, qualifications, competences, personality attributes, personal circumstances, etc.), the process is intended to assess.

Of course, unlike Norman, *you* will have read CVs or application forms from any candidates *before* any interview takes place, and determined any questions arising from the contents. These may include:

>> clarification of gaps in employment history;

>> further details in support of a candidate's suitability;

>> probing of particular areas of concern, such as salary, mobility, etc.

During the selection process, it also helps to think what information candidates will want to receive:

>> key aspects of the role, eg copy of advert;

>> some data on the location;

>> overview of selection process and timings;

>> map of location;

>> general information about the college.

In preparing for interviews, there will always be specific questions you wish to ask each particular candidate, but there is some benefit in standardising as much of the interview as possible. This makes comparisons more objective and helps to avoid the influence of the 'halo' effect (see below).

Structure

Provided that the selection interview is structured and reasonably consistent, the exact model used can remain a matter of personal style. Common approaches are:

Biographical	(*So tell me about school and university. What made you study xyz?*)
Career Path	(*Let's begin by talking about your current job, then you can tell me how your previous career led up to this*)
Competency	(*Tell me about an occasion when you have helped a member of your team improve their performance.* Or, for the admin assistant post: *Tell me how, in your previous experience, you've handled a situation where ...*)

Questioning

Use largely open questions to gather information, with occasional closed questioning to check facts or probe a particular issue.

When assessing competencies, try using 'critical incident' questions, as this challenges the candidate to talk about real life events rather than just give opinions. Wherever possible, candidates should be pressed to give examples of situations/activities from their own experience which provide evidence of what they are saying about themselves.

You may wish to challenge candidates and probe ambiguities or evasions. But avoid high pressure questioning techniques and bullying of candidates, as this rarely helps you gain the maximum information from the interviewee and damages your reputation as an employer.

Recording

You should try to record as much detail as possible of the evidence provided by the candidate during the interview, to ensure accurate assessment and allow detailed feedback to the candidate. Do this either during the interview (with the candidate's permission) or immediately afterwards.

Pitfalls

- » Legal Requirements.
    - – You must avoid discrimination on the grounds of race, colour, nationality, gender, marital status, age, sexual orientation or disability.
    - – Questioning must be directly relevant to the job and equally relevant to all candidates.
- » Personal Motivation And Emotion.

- — One is quick to perceive one's own faults in others.

- — Our expectations, realistic or otherwise, may affect our judgement.

» Abstract Characteristics.

- — You can judge verbal fluency, self-confidence, sense of humour.

- — But how will you judge honesty, integrity, sincerity?

» Non-Verbal Cues.

- — Does the body language confirm or contradict what is being said?

» Halo Effect.

- — When our judgement on a range of dimensions is swayed by a single dominant positive attribute. So instead of evaluating the person 'warts and all', the person is judged to be an all-round 'good egg'. (Once Norman knew about Olivier's army background, this candidate could do no wrong.)

» Rush to Judgement.

- — Avoid making your decision on first impressions only. First impressions stick – often regardless of later evidence. Judgements and decisions about people's characteristics are made within a matter of minutes and contradictory information is frequently ignored.

» Lack of Concentration.

- — It is very difficult to observe or listen continuously and human attention is notoriously selective. When concentration lapses we tend to reconstruct what we think we heard, or wanted to hear.

» Stereotypes.

- — Stereotypes operate when a single characteristic of an object or person brings to mind a cluster of other qualities supposedly linked to that characteristic, eg *if a person has red hair, they have a hot temper*.

» Prejudice.

- — Where you judge a person solely on the basis of a single characteristic, such as race or gender, or age. Few people can honestly claim to be free of all prejudices, so it is important that you remain self-aware (see **I is for Inclusion**).

» Attribution.

— We all have a tendency to explain our own poor performance in terms of situations and circumstances, but other people's in terms of motives and personality traits (*I lost it a bit with Angela the other evening. I'd just had a really hard week. You should have heard what she said to me, though. She hasn't half got a temper on her!*).

S is for Silver Book

Oh yes. We're open to learners 24/7. We're not on the Silver Book now, you know.

Perhaps you've heard this quaint expression and wondered in passing where it comes from. Well, if you're sitting comfortably, I'll begin. Before incorporation in 1992, lecturers' conditions of service were enshrined in a document with a silver cover, commonly referred to as the Silver Book. With incorporation came an era when individual colleges negotiated salaries and conditions with their staff. Some lecturers who declined to sign the new contracts chose instead to forego incremental rises in salary and to retain their old terms of employment, which included shorter hours and more holiday entitlement. They became known as Silver Book Lecturers. They are almost extinct now, but it is not beyond the bounds of possibility that you may encounter one still. It is rumoured that they might look poorer but not quite so exhausted as other members of your team.

S is for Stress

Always tired? Losing your temper with colleagues? Getting more headaches than usual? Losing sleep and experiencing feelings of powerlessness? Punched anyone recently who went on about teachers' holidays?

You may be suffering from undue stress. Of course, you'll have to join the queue …

What is stress?

The Health and Safety Executive defines stress as:

the adverse reaction people have to excessive pressure or other types of demand placed on them. (Accessed on 21 March 2013, *www.hse.gov.uk/stress/furtheradvice/whatisstress.htm*)

In our work and personal lives we are constantly trying to balance the demands made upon us with the internal and external resources we have to cope with them. To a degree, stress is always with us, and this is not necessarily a bad thing. Getting a bit keyed up before an important meeting or presentation may help sharpen our performance. A certain amount of pressure contributes to us getting things done on time. Some people even claim to work at their best under pressure (especially when the boss is within earshot).

However, it is the word 'excessive' which is crucial here. When the balance tips too far towards the demands placed upon us and we cannot summon the necessary resources, then we feel 'stressed' … and in a bad way.

What causes stress?

Most of us know that things like moving house, divorce and retirement, not to mention family Christmases, can be major sources of stress in our everyday lives, particularly if they all come at once. To this list we can probably add bereavement, travel, financial worries, crime and many others. But what about our working lives?

What many of the above experiences have in common is that they are often accompanied by a sense of powerlessness, an inability to determine our own fate. This is also at the root of much workplace stress. Any of these stressors sound familiar to you?

» Lack of clear objectives and values or conflicting objectives.

» Poor communication and lack of information.

» Lack of consultation or involvement in change.

» Lack of support from one's manager.

» Sustained work overload.

» Sustained work underload.

» Boring and repetitive work.

» Inadequate skills/training. Over-promotion.

» Constant dealing with complaints which one is powerless to solve.

» Career uncertainty.

» Confusing responsibilities and lines of authority.

» Lack of recognition.

» Interpersonal conflict.

What are the signs of stress?

Some signs we may only be able to recognise in ourselves. Others we can recognise in those who work for us or with us. They include:

Physical signs – like headaches, breathlessness, skin irritation, nausea or increased susceptibility to illness.

Psychological signs – like memory lapses, inability to concentrate, difficulty making decisions, bad dreams and more frequent mistakes.

Emotional signs – like irritability, moodiness, suspicion, lack of enthusiasm, loss of confidence and self-esteem, and inappropriate humour.

Behavioural changes – like loss of appetite or overeating, drinking more, smoking more, taking more work home, increased absenteeism, becoming more accident-prone, lying to cover mistakes and withdrawing from relationships.

We could all be forgiven for reading this list and concluding that not only are we highly stressed, but so are all of our work colleagues and everyone else we know. (Oh dear, was that inappropriate humour?) But everyone is different and certain personality factors may predispose a person to respond more negatively to certain stressors. The key here is to watch out for combinations of factors and for *changes*. The fact that I suffer from increasing memory lapses has been with me for some time and is probably a result of creeping senility rather than stress.

What can I do as a colleague?

Since we may all come under excessive stress at one time or another, it behoves us to look out for each other. Knowing the signs to look out for helps, but there are simple, practical things we can do as well.

- » If you notice a combination of behaviour changes, talk to the person and find out what is wrong.

- » Be supportive to those under pressure or returning after absence due to stress.

- » Set a good example in how you manage your own stress levels.

- » If you are really worried about someone, tell your manager.

What should I do as a manager?

Employers and, by extension, their managers, have a duty of care under the Health and Safety at Work Act (1974). They must take reasonable care that health is not placed at risk due to excessive and sustained levels of stress at work. Likewise, the Management of Health and Safety at Work Regulations (1999) requires managers formally to assess activities. They must ensure that the demands of the job do not exceed employees' ability to carry out the work without risk to themselves or others. If we do not, then we will lose good people and pay the price in court, as well as at work. The HSE provides guidance and management standards you can use when assessing stress in the workplace: www.hse.gov.uk/stress/standards/ and www.hse.gov.uk/stress/furtheradvice/guidance.htm (accessed on 21 March 2013).

So, for managers, there are some additional responsibilities.

- » Ensure the college has a stress policy and you know what it says, particularly about how staff voice concerns, and what counselling is available.

- » Regularly discuss performance with team members, remembering to praise them for a job well done.

- » Look at job design and workload to ensure people are given authority with responsibility, and SMART objectives (see **D is for Delegation** and **O is for Objectives**).

- » Take time to discuss personal development and training needs with individuals.

» Keep lines of communication open, and never ignore signs of stress. Make it something people can talk about, not a source of shame.

» Read your college bullying/harassment policy and ensure you avoid behaving in this way with your staff (see **B is for Bullying**).

» If you notice a combination of behaviour changes, talk to the person and find out what is wrong.

» Be supportive to those under pressure or returning after absence due to stress.

» Set a good example in how you manage your own stress levels.

What can you do about your own stress?

Clearly, because everyone is different, it is difficult to be prescriptive about what may be effective for a particular individual. But here are some ideas which seem to be broadly supported.

» Try to get a good night's sleep and stick to regular sleep patterns.

» Exercise regularly. Physical exertion can help relieve psychological stress. Try relaxation exercises.

» Watch what you eat. A healthy diet and eating regularly may help prevent stress, as will watching your caffeine and sugar intake.

» Learn to manage yourself well. Separate the important from the urgent, and schedule in reflection and planning time as well as tasks (see **T is for Time Management**).

» Take control. Ask yourself what *you* can change, and focus on that. Stop fretting about things outside your control.

» Think positive. See change as a learning opportunity.

» Take a break. Have a walk round. Freeing your mind can work wonders if you are stuck on a task.

» Get spiritual. Make time to listen to music, meditate, worship or whatever helps you wind down.

» Ask for help. Do not suffer in silence. Talk about it.

(You can find more help on this topic under **R for Resilience**.)

S is for Styles of Learning

Not everyone learns in the same way. For example, some learn better through listening to the teacher; others by engaging with a task and discovering for themselves. Most of us are *visual learners*. This means we understand and remember information best if it's presented to us as something we can see: words on a screen, pictures, diagrams, YouTube clips, real objects, and so on. *Most of us* don't learn so effectively if we only *hear* the information, although a minority of people do prefer to learn this way. They are known as *auditory learners*. And, of course, there are those who learn best through movement and activity (see **K is for Kinaesthetic Learners**). In any group of learners there is likely to be a range of these learning styles. This has obvious implications for the teacher's choice of methods and resources. Long periods of teacher talk (or *exposition*), for example, might be OK for the handful of *auditory* learners, but won't meet the needs of the visual or kinaesthetic learners in the class. To be effective, therefore, the design of a lesson plan needs to take into account this disparity of learning styles.

Much use has been made in the FE sector of the Honey and Mumford (2008) learning styles questionnaire, which identifies four main styles of learning: Reflector (learns through reflection); Theorist (most comfortable with abstract concepts); Pragmatist (learns best through experience); Activist (learns through active experience). Honey and Mumford's work is based on that of Kolb and Fry (1984), who identified four learning styles as Assimilator; Converger; Diverger; and Accommodator. However, the theory of learning styles has come under increasing criticism in academic circles recently on the grounds that any such broad categorisation is over-simplistic and can encourage teachers to think of learners as 'types' rather than individuals.

Further reading

For more on learning styles you could have a look at:

www.learning-styles-online.com/overview/

T is for Taking Responsibility

The process of colleges coming out of local authority control in the 1990s, and becoming free-standing corporations created greater accountability in individual institutions, with government openly encouraging principals to behave more like the chief executive of a business.

But is it enough simply to tell someone that they are responsible for something? Well, probably not. Like greatness, responsibility can be thrust upon you, but it generally works better if you accept, or even seek it.

The dictionary defines taking responsibility as *being answerable*, or *bound to give an explanation*. It is about taking on the task, as an individual or a team, for putting things right when they have gone wrong, but it is also about being able to take the credit when things go well. An *opting out* of responsibility might be characterised by some or all of the following:

A***-covering	*Didn't you read the e-mail?*
Invoking the mythical 'They'	*If only they would tell us what the plan is ...*
Buck-passing	*If IT had fixed my PC in time, I could have sent you those figures ...*
Jobsworthing	*It's not my job to tell them the timetable has changed ...*
Playing victim	*They want me to improve standards, but they never give me the resources to do it ...*
Coasting	*Don't worry, I'm sure somebody will already have reported that it's not working ...*

Such attitudes are easy to fall into, because we all have to work with constraints, which we may see as limiting our effectiveness. Although historically incorporation increased colleges' freedom to act, they are still dependent upon public funding which can leave them feeling under-resourced; and subject to a degree of bureaucracy from outside which may feel intrusive. So how do teachers and managers in FE set about creating the conditions for greater responsibility in their teams, and maybe adjusting to greater responsibility in their own role?

Ensure responsibility is accompanied by authority

A report by the Learning and Skills Research Centre (*Leadership, Development and Diversity in the Learning and Skills Sector*, LSRC, 2005) found that many college staff felt they had distributed *responsibility*, but not *power*. Senior management teams (SMT) regarded their style as distributed and collegiate, but those who worked for SMT often saw them as operational and transactional in their approach (see **L is for Leadership**).

Align your team behind an agreed vision and objectives

If you want people to take responsibility for decisions, and to take the initiative in improving performance, it makes sense that they must feel part of a united team. If they have had some involvement in formulating the team's vision and objectives, then the sense of ownership will be even greater. People will be more inclined to accept responsibility in pursuit of common goals, and a future which excites them.

Use measurement and standards to enable people *not* control them

It is difficult to be accountable for our performance if we have no means of measuring this. So giving people the tools to measure themselves and get reliable, meaningful feedback is essential. But people who are subjected to constant close monitoring and review from on high learn *not* to take ownership of improving their own performance. Why reflect on what you are doing and find ways to do it even better if someone is already doing this for you? The best measures and standards cover not only quantitative results but also group values and norms of behaviour. With tools like these and clearly agreed objectives, people can take responsibility for managing themselves. They are also more likely to hold each other accountable for sticking to these standards and norms.

Clarify roles and responsibilities

Not surprisingly perhaps, organisational structure can have an impact on whether people feel a clear sense of responsibility. We should avoid creating roles which have no real authority or which duplicate and interfere with each other. But it is equally important to ensure that everyone in the structure understands where their own responsibilities lie, and what responsibilities may be shared. Getting this wrong can reinforce a territorial mentality, in which managers lock themselves in their functional fortresses and pull up the drawbridge, neglecting their responsibility to help their colleagues in other teams achieve college-wide goals.

Adopt a no-blame culture

People are less inclined to take the initiative and put their head over the parapet if they think their manager is perched in the next trench with a Gatling gun. Mistakes are opportunities for the individual and the whole organisation to learn. They are also inevitable. Repeatedly making the same error is obviously to be discouraged, but organisations that adopt a problem-solving and learning approach to failure are more likely to encourage people to be accountable for their actions and decisions.

Actively promote and enable self-development

One of the things we may want people to take more responsibility for is their own development. But this does not exonerate the college from ensuring the climate, funding and processes for this to happen. Asking people to take on more or different tasks than they have in the past requires us to equip them with the tools, skills and confidence to do so.

In short, taking responsibility and improving performance need not be associated with purely transactional forms of management and close bureaucratic control. Might we actually create a greater sense of ownership by adopting some of the more involving and collaborative leadership strategies above?

T is for Teamwork

Parveen has decided to pick the brains of one of her section leaders over lunch in the local pub.

SHEENA: *Well Parveen, this is an unexpected treat! I hope you're not breaking bad news ...*

PARVEEN: *No ... Why? What have you heard? Is it about falling rolls in social care? I'm still waiting for a steer on staffing levels ...*

SHEENA: *Hey ... What? ...No, I was just kidding ... Really, go on ...*

PARVEEN: *Actually, I was rather hoping that you'd be able to help me. Jason's got this idea in his head that we're not working well together as a management team and wants us to come up with ways of being more 'teamy', whatever the hell that means. Personally, I think we all work together fine, don't you?*

SHEENA: *Err ... well ... not sure I want to answer that ... But is this what next month's trip to Forest Parks is all about?*

PARVEEN: *Yes, I mean, can you imagine? Two days stuck in a chalet with that awful woman Penny, having to appear 'teamy', while dangling from a bloody zip wire. We're going to have to wear matching cagoules, for goodness' sake! It's alright for Jason. He runs a scout troop or something ...*

SHEENA: *Actually, I think he's in the Territorials ...*

PARVEEN: *Really? Well, that would explain his bizarre obsession with starting meetings bang on time ... You've got to help me out here. Your team always seems to work really well together ...*

So, let us imagine you are Sheena. How do you begin to help your boss understand what makes for good teamwork? Given some of the clues in Parveen's anguished account, you might begin by identifying some of the obstacles that could be getting in the way of effective teamwork at the moment.

» **Lack of clarity about the team's purpose or task** Parveen does not give the impression of being well-informed about long-term strategy and goals

» **Conflicting ideas about standards of behaviour** Strong teams have agreed norms about such things as punctuality and behaviour in meetings

» **Lack of trust and fear of ridicule** Sheena's reluctance to express a view on the management team's cohesiveness and Parveen's anxieties about the great outdoors do not suggest high levels of mutual trust and respect

» **Poor understanding of colleagues' individual needs and priorities** If Parveen's understanding of her boss's needs is as good as her knowledge of his outside interests …

» **Interpersonal conflict** *That awful woman, Penny …?*

(Adapted from Downey, 2003)

So, what guidance might Sheena offer on how to avoid some of these common barriers? The first thing teams have to ensure is that they have created the right *conditions* for effective teamwork to thrive. Think about your own team. How many of these boxes could you tick?

Conditions

» Right mix of people – not just skills, but the personal strengths they bring to the team (eg as defined by personality profiles, style, or Belbin team role).

» Rapport – safe, trusting environment.

» Shared vision and team goals.

» Clear roles/responsibilities.

» Sufficient opportunity for interaction (ie we get together often enough).

» Ground rules for behaviour.

» Sense of stability/continuity.

» Freedom from chronic conflict (are there unresolved issues that must be addressed?).

The second aspect teams need to address is whether team members *behave* consistently in a way that is conducive to harmonious and productive working relationships. Once again, how many of these behaviours are demonstrated by your own team?

Behaviours

» We collaborate rather than compete.

» We are open about what we need from each other.

» We engage in constructive conflict.

» We try to help each other contribute.

» We demonstrate mutual respect.

> » We continue to learn from each other and treat mistakes as a way of doing this.

> » We observe simple social courtesies.

> » We care about each other's welfare and are supportive.

> » We keep each other 'in the loop' about what is going on.

> » We do not show favouritism.

Of course, in our rush to promote good teamwork we sometimes misconstrue what we even mean by a team. Many groups of people in organisations are exactly that; groups. A set of managers leading very different departments, with very different aims and objectives, may find it useful to meet regularly but this does not necessarily make them a team. A team can be defined as:

*A small number of people with **complementary skills**, who are **committed to a common purpose, performance goals** and **approach**, for which they hold themselves **mutually accountable**.*

(Katzenbach and Smith, 1992)

Assuming that the collection of people you lead or are a part of meet these criteria, what can you practically do to build the right kind of conditions and behaviour? Well, a spell at Forest Parks might help, if it is properly facilitated and used to address some of these key aspects of teamworking, but as an outcome of this, or any other kind of team away day, why not consider producing a team charter? This will provide a way of agreeing team purpose and goals, how communications will work, how performance will be measured, what roles people are expected to fulfil, what common standards of behaviour are important, and how conflict will be handled.

In summary, if you want your team to be seen as high-performing, then here are some of the key characteristics you will need to display.

> » PURPOSE – everyone is clear about team's work and why it's important. There is clarity around team goals.

> » ROLES – each member understands his/her role in achieving team goals.

> » FLEXIBILITY – team members perform different tasks as needed. The different strengths of individuals are used effectively.

> » HIGH STANDARDS – the whole team are committed to agreed standards of performance and behaviour.

»   PROCESSES AND POLICIES – that enable members to contribute and do their jobs easily.

»   RELATIONSHIPS – differences of opinion are valued and conflict is managed constructively. There are high levels of trust. Achievements are recognised and celebrated.

T is for Time Management

Harry has recently been given responsibility for leading the Numeracy strand of the college's Skills for Adult Learners initiative. He still has a classroom teaching workload, albeit reduced, and he is studying part-time for his Masters in Education. Here he is taking a few messages from Kimberley, the school secretary.

KIMBERLEY: *Don't rush off Harry. There's been a few phone messages for you. I don't know why they've come through to me. Is your voicemail switched on?*

HARRY: *Yes, but I've not checked it recently. Well, not since last Monday actually. Oh bugger, is it 20-past already? I'm supposed to be in Dales Court for a Standards Committee meeting. Never mind, I haven't had time to read the papers anyway. Do you think they'll miss me?*

KIMBERLEY: *They probably don't realise you're on it. You haven't been to a meeting since May.*

HARRY: *Look, I hate to ask you this, but can you do me a big favour and call Sue Graves to cancel my meeting about Learn Direct and this numeracy skills thing. I've got to prepare that communication class that Sarah asked me to do.*

KIMBERLEY: *But that's not till the end of next week, is it? You've cancelled on Sue twice already. I thought the basic skills project was your big career break?*

HARRY: *Look, I can't do everything. My desk is covered in crappy paperwork, I'm taking stuff home evenings and weekends, and I'm still letting people down. I've missed the kids' bedtimes twice this week.*

KIMBERLEY: *You do look awful.*

HARRY: *Thanks.*

KIMBERLEY: *So anyway, these messages ...*

HARRY: *Forget it. I'm off. I've got to finish this marking before 12, so I can go to something or other I've written on this sticky note and now can't bloody read. Now where did I put those assignments?*

KIMBERLEY: *Look, I'll e-mail your messages to you.*

HARRY: *Don't bother, I never get time to read my e-mails ...*

Like all of us, Harry wonders sometimes why, when technological innovation, from dishwashers to computers, claims to save us time, we seem to have even less of it than ever. Partly, it is because technology can also overload us with more information than we know what to do with. But ironically it may also be our increasing obsession with 'managing' what we see as a scarce resource, which leads us as consumers to want everything more quickly. Society demands that more get done in less time, because that is what we all want. Outside our Western corporate world, other cultures see time as plentiful. Frustrating though that may be to us in practice, this different perspective may be helpful occasionally.

Time management is a comforting, but cruelly deceptive, term. We do not really get to manage time, only manage ourselves within it. This is not about gimmicks or ready-made, near-leatherette diary systems, although they may help. It is about developing your own ways of remembering tasks, setting priorities, allocating time and avoiding wasteful activity. So, assuming we see time as in short supply, what can we do to make the most of it?

» Distinguish tasks from PURPOSE. Ask yourself, what are you here for? What really is the point of your job? What do you want from your life, and how does work fit into this? Big questions, I know, but ones Harry clearly has not thought about, which is why time pressure forces him into continuous short-term thinking. Without an overall PURPOSE decisions about priorities and objectives are built on sand.

» Agree OBJECTIVES. If these are not forthcoming, then develop your own and give them to your manager, client, partner organisation, or whatever. Make it clear this is what you will be working to, in the absence of any other input. Try to make these objectives SMART (see **O is for Objectives**).

» Distinguish EFFICIENCY from EFFECTIVENESS. Efficiency is about doing the job right, effectiveness is about doing the right job. We inevitably have to make choices about what we do. The organised people focus their efforts on doing those things which fit best with their PURPOSE and OBJECTIVES, like Harry's meeting on numeracy skills, rather than spending time, as he no doubt will, making a fantastic job of an unimportant task.

» Separate BUILDING tasks from MAINTENANCE tasks. BUILDING tasks help you to achieve your overall purpose and objectives. MAINTENANCE tasks are the million things we have to respond to every day to keep things running. If we let these take over, we get that familiar sense of working our backside off getting nowhere. Plan in time for BUILDING. Otherwise, like Harry, you will be in constant reactive mode.

» Categorise activities by URGENCY and IMPORTANCE, and then plan your time. Try to allocate at least 10–15 minutes at the start of every day to this. How many students have you urged never to begin an exam question without planning? URGENT tasks must be done quickly, but may or may not be important. IMPORTANT tasks are those which contribute to your purpose and objectives, and therefore deserve to have more time spent on them. We can see this as a matrix:

CATEGORY	NON-URGENT	URGENT
TRIVIAL	Why are you even doing this?	Do this straightaway but be careful to allocate only a small amount of time to it (or delegate)
IMPORTANT	Leave this until later but plan to spend a large chunk of time on it	Allocate a large amount of time to this immediately

Why not try analysing your current use of time by keeping a log for a few days. Then compare it to some of the points above. How are you doing? Can you consolidate more of your discretionary time, to give you space for the big important tasks?

In addition to these planning disciplines, getting more organised is about recognising and avoiding the TIME WASTERS. By this we do not mean students and colleagues, but the following sort of things:

Telephone calls

» Resist the temptation always to respond to a ringing phone. Make use of voicemail to give yourself quiet time, but ensure you regularly check messages.

» Schedule time when you're available for calls and make this clear on voicemail messages.

» Learn to say *no*.

» Avoid unstructured conversations. We've all encountered people who mistake talk for work.

» If you have the luxury of secretarial support, get calls filtered. If not, try caller recognition on your mobile.

Open door

» Don't have chairs by your desk. Face the door to see callers.

» Encourage people to make appointments.

» Schedule 'drop-in' times.

» Don't get caught in chat sessions. Tell people you are busy.

Paperwork (see **P is for Paperwork**)

» Only handle it once. Make a decision.

» Use bring-forward files to get longer-term stuff out of the way.

» Try categorising it into ACTION, INFORMATION, WASTE BIN.

» Schedule time to clear it regularly.

E-mail

» Like paperwork, take action the first time you look at it. Do not let it pile up. Respond immediately to any message you can.

» Go through it once or twice daily (not every time you get a new message alert).

» Make use of folders. Avoid printing e-mails out.

» When sending e-mails, indicate if you do not require an answer.

» Take care who you give your address to. Use spam filters.

Poor memory

» Keep up-to-date 'to-do' lists.

» Use wall planners.

» Keep a diary. Any sort you like, so long as there's only one. Block out time in it, and put in forward reminders.

Untidy desk

» Don't hoard unfinished business. For some people mess is a constant and stressful symbol of how much they have to do.

» Only have out the thing you are working on. File stuff away regularly.

Hopefully you will combine some or all of these tips into a self-organisation routine which suits you. However, better work–life balance is also about a state of mind. We do not have to get seduced into a life view that treats everything as a job to be done as quickly as possible and ticked off our to-do list. What of reflection, learning and mental and spiritual renewal? Maybe some activities lend themselves better to a more abundant view of time and a less hectic approach to the business of living (see **Y is for You**). Try to work some of this into your life as well.

(You may also want to read **D is for Delegation** and **M is for Meetings**.)

T is for Trust

So here's a word that has cropped up repeatedly in the chapters you have read so far, whether in the context of **authenticity**, **leadership**, **feedback** or a host of other aspects of your working life. Perhaps it's time we tried to pin down exactly what we mean by it.

Harry, a section leader at Bogginbrook College whom we have met before, is having one of his regular review meetings with Wayne, a newly-appointed teacher.

HARRY: *Hi Wayne, come on in. Sorry, I'm a bit late. This numeracy skills project is doing my head in. It's a bit of a mess in here, I'm afraid. I've been in meetings all week, so my marking has got a bit neglected.*

WAYNE: *Should I come back another time? I mean when there's space to sit down?*

HARRY: *No, don't worry about that. Just shove that pile onto the floor and we can sit here. I know you've been a bit concerned about things lately and the last thing I want to do is leave you in the lurch. It's important that we stick to these little sessions. I still remember how it felt to be a newbie myself. Also, I'd rather do this than face the marking ...*

WAYNE: *Thanks Harry. That's good to know, because I think I may have dropped an enormous clanger with the level 3 group.*

HARRY: *Go on.*

WAYNE: *Well, I let myself get drawn into a discussion about government policy on education, and I found myself criticising the current lot for elitism and for not understanding anything about FE because they've never even known anyone who's not been to public school, and all stuff like that. And I even started getting on my soapbox about the vocational curriculum being designed to produce a compliant workforce who can't think for themselves. I can't believe I've been so unprofessional. What am I going to do?*

HARRY: *Well, it's more a case of what you've done, isn't it, mate? You've more or less told those learners that you don't believe in what you're doing and that you don't place much value on the qualification they're working towards.*

WAYNE: *But that wasn't how I meant it. I'm on their side. You know I am.*

HARRY: *But it's not about sides, is it? It's about being professional. And sometimes that means keeping your political views to yourself. You know it was the wrong thing to do. Otherwise you wouldn't be sitting here.*

In a research report written in March 2012, the Chartered Institute of Personnel and Development (CIPD) endeavoured to identify the components of trust. What is it that makes the difference between us trusting someone to the ends of the earth and back, or not quite as far as we could throw them? CIPD identified four broad themes.

1. **Ability** – demonstrable competence at doing their job.

2. **Benevolence** – a concern for others beyond their own needs.

3. **Integrity** – adherence to a set of principles encompassing fairness and honesty (Mayer *et al.*, 1995).

4. **Predictability** – a regularity of behaviour over time (Dietz and Den Hartog, 2006).

So, how do we think Harry did? Well there is no doubt that he demonstrates a real concern for Wayne's welfare that goes beyond just a passive compliance with his formal relationship as Wayne's manager. It's also pretty clear that, with regard to his reviews with Wayne, Harry is uncharacteristically reliable and predictable. The rest of his world may be a complete shambles, but at least he prioritises his support for the new teacher. Not only that, but Harry's vagueness about his schedule, time management, marking, etc., is not reflected in his sense of right and wrong. He displays a very clear set of principles regarding professionalism, and doesn't allow Wayne to fudge the issue.

Sadly, in other respects, primarily his competence at his job, Harry makes less of a positive impression, and neglecting the prompt marking of student work, presumably as the result of chronically poor time management, is not an acceptable example to set to a newly-appointed teacher. The one redeeming feature here is that Harry is at least honest and open with Wayne about his disorganisation and dislike of marking. However, Harry still only scores three out of four. Part of good relationships at work is respect for others' ability, and the confidence that our colleagues and our managers will not let us down by dint of poor skills, whether in the classroom or the boardroom. In order earn trust, we must ensure that we perform competently and continue to update and develop our skills as our jobs change and grow.

The same CIPD report had some interesting advice for senior managers.

> » They need to demonstrate through their behaviour that they are not self-serving but serving needs of whole organisation.

Specifically they should:

> » verbally and behaviourally demonstrate greater humility;
>
> » show demonstrable respect to those at lower hierarchical levels;
>
> » display enough of their personal integrity and humanity to enable people to choose to trust them.

Above all, it is vital to ensure that the 'trust chain' is not broken. In other words, there should be consistency and honesty between senior management, local management and staff in the language and discourse concerning challenges or difficulties that the college is facing (see also **A is for Authenticity**).

It may help to see trust as like Covey's *emotional bank account* (Covey, 1989). The more you deposit, by maintaining commitments, trusting others and treating people with respect and honesty, the more you are 'in credit', and likely to be trusted yourself, even if you occasionally let people down. However, managers who manipulate and dissemble, starving their teams of information and responsibility, will find their cheque bounces when they need extra effort and support.

U is for Updating

SARAH: *Morning, Norman.*

NORMAN: *Morning, Sarah.*

SARAH: *What do you reckon to this latest White Paper on FE, then? I suppose we should have seen all that coming.*

NORMAN: *Erm … yes.*

SARAH: *It's going to mean more work.*

NORMAN: *Er … more work. Yes. Absolutely. I expect so.*

SARAH: *Although I thought on second reading that the third section seemed to hold out the promise of more funding.*

NORMAN: *Oh yes. More funding. Yeah.*

SARAH: *We'll have to have a meeting to discuss our response to paragraphs 24 and 53, I suppose. What are your first thoughts – off the top of your head?*

NORMAN: *It's … well, it's, it's absolutely what you said, isn't it.*

This scenario may be more familiar than you would like it to be. As a matter of interest, as you read it through, which of these two managers – head of school Norman, or Sarah, his head of faculty – do you find yourself empathising with? Probably neither of them. We've all met Sarah, although probably by another name. She has an uncanny ability to make you feel inadequate and borderline illiterate because she has always read every new government, Ofsted and ETF document the moment it's out, knows it by heart and can probably quote you page numbers. Where does she find the time? Does she never sleep? And we've probably all felt as Norman does here, at some time or another. You know there's something you're supposed to know, but if you ask about it, people will know you don't know.

So what's the answer to keeping updated without scaring your colleagues or giving up sleep? Some easy answers to this are:

» make sure you're on all the relevant e-mail updates lists (see the list at the end of this A–Z). You can do this by going to the appropriate Websites and registering;

» these e-mails (and the Websites) will alert you to the publication of key documents, of which you will almost always find a summary version available on the Website. The summary version may be all you need; but if not, it will guide you to the relevant sections or paragraphs you need to read in the full version;

» if you don't have time to read the education press in detail, remember that some newspapers have education supplements or pages on certain days of the week, and all of these now include FE, so that you can get the edited highlights;

» attend initiative launches and national and regional conferences when you get the chance to. The college will sometimes pay your fee and travel expenses for these. This is where you may get the opportunity to network and to hear policy in the making, and to help shape it, too;

» remember, you don't have to know everything, but you do need to be familiar with key points. You can ask colleagues who've read key documents already to let you have a bullet point list. It's generally better to say you don't know than to fake it like Norman. By pretending he knows all about the **White Paper**, he's trapped himself into a position now where he can't ask what he desperately needs to know.

Remaining updated is one of your responsibilities as a professional in FE. It's a part of your continuing professional development (CPD) in which you yourself should always be proactive. And, of course, it's also part of your responsibility to do your best to ensure that anyone you manage keeps updated, too. So don't be tempted to keep such information to yourself, nor to use it for purposes of intimidation as we suspect Sarah is doing. Knowledge may well be power, but power should not be mis-used (see **P is for Politics**).

V is for Vice Principal

As a keen professional in FE, it may be that you aspire to be a VP. It may even be that you are one already, in which case brace yourself, for you are about to read some home truths about your role.

The first and foremost of these is that the VP is very often defined in relation to the principal's management style. Whatever the job specification, if the principal's approach is warm and hands-on and he or she knows everyone on the staff by their first name, then the odds are that the VP will be squeezed into the role of hatchet-person, the hard cop, the scary one. Conversely, a principal who prefers to keep their distance, who's happier with numbers than with names, will need a VP who can exhibit the caring side of senior management, the likeable, human approach, the good cop. These are both extremes, but you get the idea. When the principal–VP team is working well, the strengths and the styles of the two will complement each other, as in any good partnership. If it isn't working well, then this is where we may encounter the interesting phenomenon of the Parked VP. The Parked VP is so called not because he or she has been put in charge of car parks (although, sadly, this has been known to be the case), but because they appear to have no vital role in the organisation structure: no line management responsibilities; no meaningful role or responsibility in relation to curriculum, funding or personnel. They have, in other words, been 'parked'. This can be an enormous and frustrating waste of management potential and talent, engineered by an over-mighty principal, a misguided Board, or an inappropriate organisational structure. Or it could be a strategy utilised to accommodate a VP who has not lived up to their original promise. Whatever the case, it will be clear from this that a great deal can be learned about the way a college is managed from looking at the role of its VP.

OK, VPs. Open your eyes. You can start reading again now.

V is for VLEs and Other Learning Technologies

A virtual learning environment (VLE) is a software tool which enables learners to access learning materials, engage in group discussions, maintain contact with their teacher and submit their work for assessment via a 'dropbox' function. It is a learning *resource*, rather than a learning method, offering learners an additional source of support and contact. It is just one manifestation of what is more broadly known as e-learning – learning facilitated by computer technology – which may include the use of the internet, the college's intranet or Website, or subject-specific software.

E-learning is, of course, an abbreviation of electronic learning. One of its most useful applications is in distance learning, sometimes described as asynchronous distributed learning: *asynchronous* because learners are accessing the learning site at different times; and *distributed* because the learners are located at different places. There are other specialised terms, too. For example, a discussion held online is known as a *threaded discussion* because each individual learner's contribution can be 'unpicked', tracked and assessed. E-learners may be referred to as *participants* rather than students and the teacher or facilitator is sometimes known as the *e-moderator*, a term used in the title of G. Salmon's useful book for teachers, *E-moderating: The Key to Online Teaching and Learning*. When e-learning, such as that provided via VLE, is combined with traditional face-to-face delivery, this is known as a *blended learning* model.

Although e-learning can be extremely useful, allowing learners to study at a distance or at times that suit them best, it can, when used alone, have certain disadvantages. Learners may feel isolated; they may find asynchronous online discussion less engaging than face-to-face interaction with teachers or peers. Research suggests that non-completion and dropout rates for online courses are generally higher than for those requiring attendance. With this in mind, the emphasis for the teacher should be on maintaining regular contact with learners and providing them with appropriate tutorial support. Perhaps the most important thing to remember is that learning technologies – whether we're talking about VLEs, interactive whiteboards, data projectors, teacher tweets or college blogs – are tools or resources for teachers to use. Ideally, they should contribute to good teaching rather than be used as a substitute for it.

Further reading

If you are supporting learners online you will find the following book useful:

Salmon, G. (2004) *E-moderating: The Key to Online Teaching and Learning* (3rd Edition). Abingdon: Routledge.

Salmon, G. (2013) *E-tivities: The Key to Active Online Learning* (2nd Edition). Abingdon: Routledge.

W is for Walking Around

The simple idea of 'management by walking around' has been written about by numerous authors on leadership and management over the last century, not least the renowned Peter Drucker; but it is certain that the practice has been around a lot longer than this.

It may seem a statement of the obvious to suggest that managing people well involves getting off your behind and talking to them where they work, rather than always expecting them to come to you. But it is surprising how we can be seduced into spending most of our time on the things we purport to hate – answering e-mails, doing paperwork, sitting in meetings – rather than getting out there and talking to our team. Having an 'open-door policy' just doesn't cut it. Why should your team walk through this 'open door' if you cannot find the time to walk through in the opposite direction?

Of course, we are not all sociable extraverts by nature, who find this walking around chatting to people easy. It may feel quite a challenge, even uncomfortable. But experience suggests that this is a management behaviour which is appreciated even when done badly, provided your motives are positive. People like to see their boss making the effort, even if it does not come naturally.

Let's look at some of the things walking around allows a manager to do.

>   Be a visible role model.

>   Show people you are interested in what they are doing and thinking.

>   Take the opportunity to listen, praise and encourage.

>   Observe the social courtesies. Ask after family. Talk about holidays.

>   Be accessible and approachable.

>   Answer people's questions. Reassure if possible.

>   Reinforce the team's purpose and objectives.

>   Identify conflict early and address appropriately.

>   Keep learning yourself.

But beware; this is a behaviour that has to be practised consistently, in order to be effective. It is an especially helpful form of communication in times of great change; it is true. But if you only walk around and talk to people in times of great change, your team will, in the manner of Pavlov's dogs, associate your visibility with bad news. Likewise, if your motivation for walking around is to spy on people and catch them up to no good, you will lose the trust and respect of your team, rather than encourage it. Think Henry V, rather than J. Edgar Hoover:

> *O! now, who will behold*
> *The royal captain of this ruined band*
> *Walking from watch to watch, from tent to tent,*
> *Let him cry 'Praise and glory on his head!'*
> *For forth he goes and visits all his host,*
> *Bids them good morrow, with a modest smile,*
> *And calls them brothers, friends and countrymen.*
>
> (From the prologue to Act IV, *Henry V*, by William Shakespeare)

W is for White Papers and Other Milestones

Over the past three decades the changes to the organisation, curriculum, funding and inspection of FE colleges have brought about a radical and rapid transformation of the sector. We can track these changes by looking back over the White and Green Papers, the reports and the initiatives that have triggered or signalled each new development. In this A–Z we have picked the **Foster Report** out for special mention, but some other major milestones have been:

»   *Working Together: Education and Training* (1986): this White Paper introduced NVQs (National Vocational Qualifications) in order to rationalise the existing complex range of qualifications into a coherent framework with comparable national benchmarks;

»   *Education and Training for the 21st Century* (1991): this White Paper signalled the removal of colleges from local authority control; the beginnings of incorporation; the introduction of GNVQs (General Vocational Qualifications); and the potential for schools to compete with colleges in the provision of vocational education;

»   *The Dearing Review of Post-16 Qualifications* (1996): the recommendations were to preserve A levels and the general/vocation divide, and to introduce key skills across the post-16 curriculum;

»   *The Tomlinson Report* (1996): a milestone in the implementation of Inclusive Learning;

»   *The Learning Age* (1998): set the target that all FE lecturers should undertake a professional teaching qualification. This initiative was to be supported by the FE Standards Fund;

»   *Learning to Succeed* (1999): signalled the setting up of the national and regional LSCs (Learning and Skills Councils) and their crucial role in the funding of FE (including administering the Standards Fund);

»   *Success for All* (2002): a reform strategy to develop the responsiveness of the FE sector and other lifelong learning providers, with an emphasis on working with employers, 'busting bureaucracy', encouraging equality and diversity, and developing e-learning;

» *Every Child Matters* (2003): this Green Paper has had an impact on all sectors of education, with its focus on: supporting parents and carers; workforce reform; encouraging accountability and integration between services and institutions; and early intervention for the protection of young people at risk;

» *14–19 Education and Skills* (2005): not all proposals of this White Paper survived a subsequent change of government, but they included: the remotivation of disengaged 14-year-olds by allowing them to learn in FE colleges; a mastery of functional English and mathematics by all young people before they leave education; and the introduction of Diplomas in 14 broad vocational areas, designed by employers through Sector Skills Councils;

» *Further Education: Raising Skills, Improving Life Chances* (2006): containing the government response to the Foster Report, this White Paper also included new entitlements for 19–25-year-olds studying for their first level 3 qualification, and the proposal that all new college principals should gain a leadership qualification.

You will find a list of sources at the end of this A–Z which will help you to continue your professional **updating** about future initiatives, White Papers and other publications.

(See also **E is for ETF**.)

X is for X-Men

X-women? X-men? OK, so now we're really getting desperate. Still, anything has got to be better than appalling puns about X-cellence or X-pertise; and basing a taxonomy of teaching and management styles around fictional superheroes is not that crazy an idea. We would like to bet that you recognise some of these colleagues, even if you would be well-advised not to emulate them.

STORM: *Flies all over the place, generating wind and fog.*

PROFESSOR X: *Communicates by telepathy. Will expect you therefore to know what he's thinking.*

ROGUE: *Drains the life-force out of anyone she comes into contact with.*

ICEMAN: *Can reduce temperatures to sub-zero, just by walking into a room.*

WOLVERINE: *Poor emotional control and, when enraged (which is often), the claws really come out. Also, rather depressingly, he is virtually indestructible.*

Y is for You

You'll be a more effective practitioner if you make space to look after your own professional and personal needs.

» Take time occasionally to think about what *you* want, where you're heading, and how this fits with your hopes and aspirations. Are you where you want to be? If not, what's the first step to getting there?

» Leave room for real life. There's more to life than work, although sometimes in FE it's easy to forget this. It's important to ring-fence time – an evening or at weekends – when you not only don't talk about work but don't even *think* about it. Don't get yourself stuck into a regime of working where you have to remind your family and friends what your name is.

Z is for Zero-Tolerance

Save your zero-tolerance for the big things. As a professional in FE you should demonstrate a zero-tolerance of:

- » bullying;
- » discrimination;
- » harassment;
- » unprofessional behaviour;
- » illegal practices;
- » corruption;
- » dishonesty;
- » exploitation.

A policy of zero-tolerance will be pointless, of course, if you're seen to tolerate any of these behaviours in yourself.

And Finally ... P is for Postscript

A final word. This book has hopefully succeeded in giving you a very brief introduction to a lot of the things that will give you fun-filled days, and maybe some sleepless nights, as a teacher or manager in FE. It would be easy to get overwhelmed by the sheer volume of activities, techniques, initiatives and procedures. So, here's a very simple, last piece of advice. A cursory glance down the contents list of this A–Z reveals that well over 50 per cent of the topics we cover are, in essence, about your relationships with people, and how to make these more productive. The desire and ability to really connect with people is probably the aspect of teaching and leadership that we would most want to emphasise. Ultimately, your success as a professional will depend largely on getting the best out of others, whether they are your team, your colleagues, or your boss.

Like anyone else, you will sometimes come home feeling frustrated and fed-up, certain you have made enemies of everyone, and wasted your considerable talents on fruitless bureaucracy and 'politicking'. But, with any luck, you will have far more good days than bad. And on those days you will come home, feeling elated and fulfilled, certain that you have really contributed to the vision of the college, and made a real, positive difference in people's lives.

Useful references

Adair, J. (1983) *Effective Leadership*. London: Gower.

Alexander, C. (1999) *'Endurance': Shackleton's Legendary Journey to Antarctica*. London: Bloomsbury.

Avolio, B.J. (1999) *Full Leadership Development: Building the Vital Forces in Organizations*. Thousand Oaks: Sage.

Baguley, P. (2002) *Teach Yourself Teams and Team-Working*. McGraw-Hill Companies.

Barrett, R. (1998) *Liberating the Corporate Soul*. Woburn: Butterworth-Heinemann.

Bass, B.M. (1998) *Transformational Leadership: Industrial, Military and Educational Impact*. Mahwah: Erlbaum.

Bennis, W.G. (1989) *On Becoming a Leader*. London: Random House.

Bennis, W.G. and Thomas, R.J. (2002) *Geeks & Geezers*. Boston: Harvard Business School Press.

Blanchard, K., Zigarmi, P. and Zigarmi, D. (1986) *Leadership and the One-Minute Manager*. London: Collins.

Bolman, L. and Deal, T. (1993) *Reframing Organizations: Artistry, Choice and Leadership*. San Francisco: Jossey-Bass.

Bridges, W. (1991) *Managing Transitions*. Reading, MA: Perseus.

Clutterbuck, D. (2007) *Coaching the Team at Work*. London: Nicholas Brealey International.

Cottrell, S. (2011) *Critical Thinking Skills*. Abingdon: Routledge.

Covey, S.R. (1989) *The Seven Habits of Highly Effective People*. London: Simon & Schuster.

DES (1991) *Education and Training for the 21st Century*. London: HMSO.

Dietz, G. and Den Hartog, D.N. (2006) Measuring Trust inside Organisations. *Personnel Review*, 35(5): 557 88.

Downey, M. (2003) *Effective Coaching*. New York: Thomson Texere.

Drucker, P.F. (2001) *The Essential Drucker*. Woburn: Butterworth-Heinemann.

Ellis, A. (1999) *How to Make Yourself Happy*. Atascadero: Impact Publishers.

Etzioni, A. (1961) *A Comparative Analysis of Complex Organizations: On Power, Involvement, and their Correlates*. New York: Free Press of Glencoe.

Firth, D. (1999) *Smart Things to Know About Change*. Oxford: Capstone.

Gladwell, M. (2000) *The Tipping Point*. London: Little, Brown and Company.

Goleman, D. (1996) *Emotional Intelligence*. London: Bloomsbury.

Goleman, D. (1998) *Working with Emotional Intelligence*. London: Bloomsbury.

Handy, C. (1995) *Gods of Management: The Changing Work of Organisations*. London: Arrow.

Handy, C. (1999) *Understanding Organisations*. London: Penguin.

Hatch, M.J. (1997) *Organization Theory*. Oxford: Oxford University Press.

Hope-Hailey, V., Searle, R. and Dietz, G., with help from Abbotson, S., Robinson, V., McCartney, C. and Wright, B. (2012) *Where Has All the Trust Gone?* London: CIPD.

Kanter, R. (1983) *Changemasters*. Abingdon: Routledge.

Katzenbach, J.R. and Smith, D.K. (1992) *The Wisdom of Teams*. Harvard Business School Press.

Kolb, D. (1983) *Experiential Learning*. Hemel Hempstead: Prentice Hall.

Kotter, J.P. (1996) *Leading Change*. Boston: Harvard Business School Press.

Landsberg, M. (1996) *The Tao of Coaching*. London: HarperCollins.

Lee, S. and Kirby, J. (1963) *X-Men*. New York: Marvel Comics.

Leigh, A. (1984) *20 Ways to Manage Better*. London: CIPD.

Lumby, J., Harris, A., Morrison, M., Mujis, D., Sood, K., Glover, D., Wilson, M., Briggs, A.R.J. and Middlewood, D. (2005) *Leadership, Development and Diversity in the Learning and Skills Sector*. London: Learning and Skills Research Centre.

MacLeod, D. and Clarke, N. (2011) Engaging for Success: Enhancing Performance through Employee Engagement. A report to government.

Maslow, A. (1987) *Motivation and Personality*. London: Harper & Row.

Mayer, R.C., Davis, J.H. and Schoorman, F.D. (1995) An Integrative Model of Organizational Trust. *Academy of Management Review*, 20: 709–34.

Mehrabian, A. (1972) *Silent Messages: Implicit Communication of Emotions and Attitudes*. Belmont: Wadsworth Publishing Company.

Morgan, G. (1998) *Images of Organization*. Thousand Oaks: Sage.

Morrell, M. and Capparell, S. (2001) *Shackleton's Way*. London: Nicholas Brealey Publishing.

Owen, J. (2002) *Benchmarking for the Learning and Skills Sector*. LSDA.

Peart, S. (2012) *Making Education Work: How Black Men and Boys Navigate the Further Education Sector*. London: Trentham.

Pemberton, C. (2006) *Coaching to Solutions*. Oxford: Elsevier Ltd.

Pring, R. (1999) *Closing the Gap: Liberal Education and Vocational Preparation*. London: Hodder & Stoughton.

Robinson, D. (2008) Employee Engagement: An IES Perspective. Presentation to the IES HR Network.

Rogers, A. and Horrocks, N. (2010) *Teaching Adults* (4th Edition). *Maidenhead*: Open University Press.

Ryff, C.D. (1989) Happiness is Everything, or is it? Explorations on the Meaning of Psychological Well-being. *Journal of Personality and Social Psychology*, 57(6): 1069–81.

Salmon, G. (2004) *E-moderating: The Key to Teaching and Learning Online*. London: Kogan Page.

Sandel, M.J. (2013) *What Money Can't Buy: The Moral Limits of Markets*. London: Penguin Books.

Schein, E. (1969) *Process Consultation: Its Role in Organisation Development*. Reading, MA: Addison Wesley Publishing.

Schein, E. (1992) *Organisational Culture & Leadership*. San Francisco: Jossey-Bass.

Seligman, M. (2011) *Flourish*. London: Nicholas Brealey Publishing.

Senge, P. (1990) *The Fifth Discipline*. London: Random House.

Sung, J. and Ashton, D.N. (2005) *Achieving Best Practice in Your Business. High Performance Work Practices: Linking Strategy and Skills to Performance Outcomes*. London: Department of Trade and Industry in association with CIPD.

Torrington, D. *et al.* (2001) *Human Resource Management*. London: Prentice Hall.

Tummons, J. (2011) *Assessing Learning in the Lifelong Learning Sector* (2nd Edition). Exeter: Learning Matters.

Wallace, S. (2007) *Getting the Buggers Motivated in FE*. London: Continuum.

Wallace, S. (2011) *Teaching, Tutoring and Training in the LLS* (4th Edition). Exeter: Learning Matters.

Wallace, S. (2013) *Managing Behaviour in FE* (3rd Edition). London: Sage/Learning Matters.

Wallace, S. and Gravells, J. (2005) *Mentoring in Further Education*. Exeter: Learning Matters.

West, M.A. (2004) *Effective Teamworking*. Oxford: BPS & Blackwell Publishing Ltd.

Whitmore, J. (1992) *Coaching for Performance*. London: Nicholas Brealey Publishing.

Useful websites

ACAS Website (harassment/bullying): www.acas.org.uk/index.aspx?articleid=797 (accessed on 3 July 2013).

ACAS Website (disciplinary process):

www.acas.org.uk/media/pdf/k/b/Acas_Code_of_Practice_1_on_disciplinary_and_grievance_procedures-accessible-version-Jul-2012.pdf

(accessed on 28 June 2013).

Health and Safety Executive Website (stress):

www.hse.gov.uk/stress/standards/ and www.hse.gov.uk/stress/furtheradvice/guidance.htm

www.hse.gov.uk/stress/furtheradvice/whatisstress.htm

(accessed on 21 March 2013).

Useful sources for updating

In the section on **Updating** we suggested that you consult key Websites to keep yourself up-to-date with current developments. The following bodies and organisations all have useful Websites which you can access through the search engine of your choice. Some even have 'mailing lists' which allow you to sign up for regular e-mail updates:

» the DfE (Department for Education);

» the Association of Colleges (AoC);

» the Education and Training Foundation (ETF);

» the University and College Union (UCU);

» the National Institute of Adult Continuing Education (NIACE);

» the Institute for Learning (IfL);

» *The Times Educational Supplement* (TES);

» the *Guardian* education pages.